MARY IN THE DOCUMENTS
OF THE CHURCH

MARY
IN THE DOCUMENTS
OF THE CHURCH

By
PAUL F. PALMER, S.J., S.T.D.

with a Word to the Reader by
GERALD G. WALSH, S.J., Ph.D.

LONDON
BURNS OATES
1953

11284

Imprimi potest
JOANNES J. McMAHON, S.J.
Praepositus Provincialis
Provinciae Neo-Eboracensis

Nihil obstat
E. A. CERNY, S.S., D.D.
Censor librorum

Imprimatur
FRANCISCUS P. KEOUGH, D.D.
Archiepiscopus Baltimorensis
die 23 mensis Novembris 1951

MADE AND PRINTED IN GREAT BRITAIN BY
LOWE AND BRYDONE (PRINTERS) LTD., LONDON, N.W.10, FOR
BURNS OATES AND WASHBOURNE LTD.,
28 ASHLEY PLACE, LONDON, S.W.1

EDITOR'S FOREWORD

★

For some years now the editor has been preparing a series of volumes in documentary form to illustrate the basic dogmas of the Christian faith in the light of their historical development. While he was readying a volume to be entitled *Mary, the Second Eve*, the Holy See solemnly defined the dogma of our Lady's Assumption into heaven. In view of the interest that this proclamation awakened even in non-Catholic circles, it was decided to edit as a completely separate work the present small volume under the title *Mary in the Documents of the Church*.

The documents are drawn principally from the early ecclesiastical writers and Fathers of the Church, from the creeds and canons of ecumenical councils, and from the official pronouncements of the Holy See. Parts I to IV bear witness to a Marian tradition that is the common heritage of the great Churches of the East and the West up to the period of the disastrous Eastern schism under Photius, Patriarch of Constantinople (858–67), although the last Eastern writer to be cited is St. John Damascene (d. 749), recognized by the East and the West as the last of the Greek Fathers. Damascene's eloquent testimony to the Immaculate Conception and to the bodily Assumption of our Lady into heaven has so fixed these doctrines in the minds of Eastern Christians that the editor has felt free to consider thereafter the less tranquil development of these same dogmas in the Church of the West.

The editor did not feel qualified to trace the development of Mariology in Anglican and Protestant theology. Generally speaking, the theologians of these Churches maintain that all development or explication of doctrine was arrested or came to an end by the time of the fourth or the sixth ecumenical councils—that of Chalcedon (451) or that of Constantinople (the third to be held there, 681). If this be so, then Anglicans and Protestants will find in this brief study sufficient illustration of their own tradition on Mary the Virgin. Faced with this tradition, they may continue to challenge the right of the pope of Rome to pronounce dogmatically on the theology of Mary, but surely they will be more reluctant to challenge the truth of the doctrines proclaimed. And this very real step in the direction of Christian unity may hasten the day when Christians once again can call upon Mary as the Mother of Christians, without adding those divisive qualifiers which are now so necessary to distinguish them.

PAUL F. PALMER, S.J.

A WORD TO THE READER

★

Neither the simplest discussion, however friendly, nor the most learned debate, however acrimonious, between Catholic and non-Catholic Christians could even begin, let alone continue, without a common theological vocabulary. Nouns like *Trinity, Incarnation, Redemption, predestination* and *transubstantiation*, which name but a few of the incomprehensible "mysteries" of faith; adjectives like *supernatural, theandric, hypostatical, sacramental* and *eschatological*, which serve as a kind of theological shorthand; names of the great systematic cleavages—*Catholicism, Orthodoxy* and *Protestantism*—and of the lesser sectarian differences—*Lutheranism, Calvinism, Methodism*—these terms and hundreds of others dot, and must dot, all Christian conversations.

Yet, not one of these words appears in any of the four Gospels. They arose in the course of Christian discussions which are now a matter of history, and they serve as useful summaries of significant crises in Christian development. It may be debated whether, in all cases, they are the best words for the purpose. Thus it might be argued that, although *Incarnation* (Latin *caro*, flesh) recalls the Biblical expression, "The Word became flesh" (John 1:14), yet the form familiar to the Greek Fathers, *enanthropesis* (*anthropos*, man), is a better summary of the point at issue. Happily, however, the history of the words is known to most of the serious scholars and, therefore, the choice of this or that word is of less importance.

Take a word like *supernatural*. It is relatively a late-comer in the history of theology. Not only did our Lord not use the word, but not even did that great giant of patristic theology, St. Augustine of Hippo (354–430). Every student of St. Augustine's works has regretted this latter fact. In connection with such indeterminate words as *virtue* and *good*, the presence of a qualifying *supernatural* would have cleared up hundreds and hundreds of doubts and have saved Christian discussion from an incalculable amount of theological acerbity. When sober scholarship finally succeeds in convincing us all that the contexts have been discovered where the word is indubitably needed, a long step, under God, will have been taken in the direction of something like the beginning of a Catholic-Lutheran concord.

Now, one of the main values of Father Palmer's work lies, it seems to me, in the history of theological vocabulary. He limits himself to the demonstration of the gradual and continuous development of a vocabulary appropriate to the theological implications in the Biblical revelation connected with "Mary, the mother of Jesus" (John 2:3). Like the gospel revelation concerning the Trinity. that concerning Mary is relatively slight but immensely significant. One has only to read the passage beginning "The angel Gabriel was sent by God" (Luke 1:26 ff.) to realize that one is in the presence of divine communications the like of which appear nowhere else in the whole history of revelation. Mary's connection with the mystery of the Incarnation is revealed as inexpressibly and even incomprehensibly close—so close, in fact, that, had the Church of the ghettoes and the catacombs been able to produce a profound theologian endowed with the intuitive sense of a great historian, he could have predicted that, once the inspired intelligence of the Church had devised the right vocabulary to deal with the Trinitarian and Incarnational heresies, there would be need to deal in the same way with the logically inevitable attacks on, or misunderstandings of, the revelation concerning "Mary, the mother of Jesus."

That, in historical fact, was the sequence in which the heresies came. As soon as Gnosticism—the most fundamental of all heresies in the sense that it is, radically, a substitution of human reasoning for divine revelation—had been dealt with, attention had to be given, from the end of the second century on, to the anti-Trinitarians; then in the fourth century, to the Arian and Apollinarian attacks on the full reality of the Incarnation; and, finally, by a logic of facts which is as inexorable as in secular history, to the Nestorian attack on "Mary, the mother of Jesus."

As Father Palmer well puts it, "any caricature of the Son would involve a caricature of the Mother." That is why it was important here to have documentation going back as far as the Creed of Hippolytus and even to the letter of St. Ignatius of Antioch to the Trallians, written in the first decade of the second century. In a sense, the key document is the first anathema of St. Cyril against Nestorius, which officially and authoritatively put the word *Theotokos* (Mother of God) into the lexicon of Christian theology. All the subsequent documentation serves merely to explicate the implications of Ephesian Mariology. Some of these implications had, of course, long since been made explicit, as can be seen, for example, by what St. Irenaeus had written in the third quarter of the second century (p. 13) and what St. Hippolytus had said in the first half of the third century (p..15).

There are documents here which should appeal to all who feel the force of that poetry of faith or "Inner Light"—to use a later expression of the Society of Friends—which has played a not insignificant role in enriching our Christian vocabulary. From this point of view, though not only from this point of view, the hymns of St. Ephrem the Syrian will be read and meditated with delight. Christian poetry, as poetry, did not reach its culmination here; but the dogmatic value of Ephrem is, of course, far beyond that of Dante. Nevertheless, I should have been glad to see included here—if only it were to the editor's purpose, and a translation worthy of the original were available—Bernard's Prayer to the Virgin in the thirty-third canto of the *Paradiso*, including the poet's firm profession of faith in Mary as the Mediatrix of grace.

The debate over expressions like *Immaculate Conception* and *Assumption* continues long after the debate over *Mother of God* was settled at Ephesus (431), just as the debate over *Theotokos* continued for a century after the Council of Nicaea (325) had given us the word *homoousios* (consubstantial). This little collection of documents, with its rigorously historical criteria and its minimum of theological intrusion, will, please God, help many minds to deal with the contemporary debates more intelligently and, perhaps, in a more Christian spirit than they have ever done before.

GERALD G. WALSH, S.J.

ACKNOWLEDGMENTS

★

The style and arrangement of this book follow closely the Galaxy edition of Henry Bettenson's *Documents of the Christian Church*, Oxford University Press, 1947. Unless credit is otherwise given, the translations are the responsibility of the editor. The editor has, however, based his own translations on those of others, where such exist, and, with the exception of the Syrian hymns of St. Ephrem, has checked all translations against their originals as these are found in the best edited texts. In this painstaking task, not always within his easy competence, the editor has had the assistance of his colleague, Walter J. Burghardt, S.J., professor of patrology and patristic theology at Woodstock College, Maryland.

The titles listed below under "Abbreviations" show the sources from which the editor has made his selections. A special note of thanks, moreover, is due the following publishers for their permission to use copyright passages:

The Newman Press, Westminster, Maryland (*Ancient Christian Writers*).

The Fathers of the Church, Inc. (*The Fathers of the Church*).

Blackfriars Publications, Oxford ("The Akathistos Hymn").

CONTENTS

★

PART III

THE TRADITION OF THE WEST

PART IV

DEVOTION TO MARY IN THE EAST

PART V

CONTROVERSY IN THE WEST

PART IX

THE DOGMA OF THE ASSUMPTION

Pius XII: Apostolic Constitution "Munificentis-
simus Deus," Nov. 1, 1950

ABBREVIATIONS

★

AAS   *Acta apostolicae sedis, commentarium officiale*, Rome, 1909–

ACO   *Acta conciliorum oecumenicorum*, ed. Schwartz; Berlin and Leipzig, 1914 ff.

ACW   *Ancient Christian Writers*, ed. Quasten-Plumpe; Westminster, Maryland, 1946–

AP   *Pii IX pontificis maximi acta*, Rome, 1854 ff.

ASS   *Acta sanctae sedis*, Rome, 1865 ff.

CSEL   *Corpus scriptorum ecclesiasticorum latinorum*, Vienna Academy; Vienna, 1866 ff.

DB   Denzinger-Banwart, *Enchiridion symbolorum, definitionum et declarationum de rebus fidei et morum*, ed. 24–25 by Umberg; Barcelona, 1948.

DTC   *Dictionnaire de théologie catholique*, ed. Vacant-Mangenot; Paris, 1903–

FC   *The Fathers of the Church*, ed. Schopp, Deferrari; New York, 1946–

GCS   *Die Griechischen Christlichen Schriftsteller*, Leipzig, 1897 ff.

Harvey   Harvey, W. W., *S. Irenaei libri 5 adversus haereses*, 2 vols., Cambridge, 1857.

Lamy   Lamy, T. J., *Sancti Ephraem Syri hymni et sermones*, 4 vols., Mechlin, 1882–92.

Livius   Livius, Thomas, *The Blessed Virgin in the Fathers of the First Six Centuries*, London, 1893.

NPN   *The Nicene and Post-Nicene Fathers*, Oxford, 1894.

PG   *Patrologia, series graeca*, ed. Migne; Paris, 1844 ff.

PL   *Patrologia, series latina*, ed. Migne; Paris, 1857 ff.

Multa quippe ad fidem catholicam pertinentia, dum haereticorum calida inquietudine exagitantur, ut adversus eos defendi possint, et considerantur diligentius et intelliguntur clarius et instantius praedicantur, et ab adversario mota quaestio discendi existit occasio.

For there are many points of the Catholic faith which, when put on the defensive by the restless zeal of heresy, come to be examined with more thoroughness, grasped with more clarity, and proclaimed with more emphasis. Thus does doubt, raised by the adversary, end in dogma.

St. Augustine: *The City of God*, XVI, 2
(CSEL, 2, 124–25).

MARY IN THE DOCUMENTS
OF THE CHURCH

PART I

THE FAITH OF THE EARLY CHURCH

[Until the Council of Ephesus (431) the Church was engaged principally in the refutation of the great Trinitarian heresies. These denied in turn the trinity of Persons (Sabellianism, c. 220), the unity of the divine nature (Tritheism, c. 260), the divinity of the Son (Arianism, c. 320) and the divinity of the Holy Spirit (Macedonianism, c. 380). And yet, if we go back to the early decades of Christianity, to the days when the question "What think ye of Christ?" was first being put to the pagans, we find a group on the fringe of the Christian community that denied not so much the divinity of Christ as His humanity. Docetists by name, they denied that the "Word was made flesh," and, by implication, that the Virgin Mary was the real mother of Jesus. For, intimately associated as Mary is with her Son, it was inevitable that any caricature of the Son would involve a caricature of the Mother. Two centuries later, the Arians, by denying that the Son was really God, implicitly denied that Mary was the Mother of God. Thus, it was impossible to attack either the humanity or the divinity of the God-Man without denying Mary's greatest of privileges, her divine motherhood. Conversely, as Nestorius discovered at the Council of Ephesus, it was impossible to question Mary's right to the title *Theotokos* (Mother of God), without denying the divinity of her Son. For these reasons, the Church in her liturgy addresses Mary: "Thou alone hast overcome all heresies."]

3

1. Mary in the Apostles' Creed

[The Creed attributed by Rufinus (c. 400) to the Apostles can be traced back to the time of St. Hippolytus (d. 236). With slight modifications it forms the Baptismal Creed of the Roman Church, and may well be a century old when Hippolytus records it in his *Apostolic Tradition*. The Creed itself is an explicit statement of the belief of the primitive Church in Mary as Virgin and Mother of Jesus, who is the Son of God. It is in the Christological (dealing with Christ) section of the Creed, which emphasizes both the divinity and the humanity of Jesus, that Mary comes to the fore. The first four articles of the Creed are given as they are found in Rufinus and in Hippolytus.]

a. The Creed of Rufinus, c. 400

I believe in God the Father Almighty,
and in Christ Jesus His only Son, our Lord,
who was born from the Holy Spirit and the Virgin
     Mary,
who was crucified under Pontius Pilate, and buried . . .

The Apostolic Symbol or *Creed* (DB, 2).

b. The Creed of Hippolytus, c. 215

Dost thou believe in God the Father Almighty? . . .
Dost thou believe in Christ Jesus, the Son of God,
who was born by the Holy Spirit from the Virgin
     Mary,
who was crucified under Pontius Pilate, and died. . . .

The Apostolic Tradition of St. Hippolytus,
XXI, 12, 15 (ed. Gregory Dix, p. 26).

2. Early Heresies Involving Mary

a. Docetism. St. Ignatius of Antioch, c. 110

[St. Ignatius on his way to Rome and martyrdom warns the Christians of Tralles against the Docetists (Gk. *dokein,* to appear, to make believe). These early heretics, who exaggerated the spirit at the expense of matter, held that Christ's body was but a phantom, that His birth, suffering and death were only apparent or make-believe. St. Ignatius' implicit reference to the Apostles' Creed would indicate the sect against which the Christological section of the Creed was first directed.]

Stop your ears therefore when anyone speaks to you that stands apart from Jesus Christ, from David's scion and Mary's Son, who was really born and ate and drank, really persecuted by Pontius Pilate, really crucified and died while heaven and earth and the underworld looked on; who also really rose from the dead, since His Father raised Him up—His Father, who will likewise raise up all who believe in Him through Jesus Christ, apart from whom we have no real life.

But if, as some atheists, that is, unbelievers, say, His suffering was but a make-believe—when in reality, they themselves are make-believes—why then am I in chains? Why do I even pray that I may fight wild beasts? In vain, then, do I die! My testimony is, after all, but a lie about the Lord!

To the Trallians, 9–10 (ed. Funk-Bihlmeyer; tr. J. Kleist, ACW, 1, 77–78).

b. Gnosticism. St. Irenaeus, c. 177

[There are two forms of Gnosticism: the Docetist type denies that the Savior was born of Mary; the Judaizing type regards Jesus as an ordinary man, born of Mary and Joseph.]

He [Saturninus, c. 120] declared that the Savior was unborn, incorporeal and without form (and that He was seen) as a man only in appearance. . . . He was the first to say that the angels fashioned two kinds of men, one bad, the other good. . . . But to marry and bear children they say is of Satan.

Against Heresies, 1, 24, 2 (Harvey,
1, 197–98; PG, 7, 674–75).

He [Cerinthus, c. 170] also said that Jesus was not born of a virgin but was the son of Joseph and Mary, like all the rest of men, only surpassing all others in justice, prudence and wisdom; that after His baptism Christ descended upon Him in the form of a dove . . . but that in the end Christ withdrew from Jesus, and Jesus suffered and rose again, while Christ remained impassable since He was by nature spiritual.

Against Heresies, 1, 26, 1 (Harvey,
1, 211–12; PG, 7, 686).

c. Arianism. The Council of Nicaea, 325

[Arianism is strictly a Trinitarian heresy which attacks the divinity of the Son, the second Person of the Trinity.

Implicitly, however, the divinity of the God-Man is denied and consequently Mary's privilege as Mother of God. We cite only the pertinent section of the Creed of Nicaea.]

We believe in one God the Father Almighty, maker of all things visible and invisible.

And in one Lord Jesus Christ, the Son of God, begotten of the Father, only-begotten, that is of the substance of the Father, God of God, Light of Light, true God of true God, begotten not made, of the same substance [consubstantial] with the Father, through whom all things were made, things in heaven and things on earth.

Who for us men and for our salvation came down and was made flesh, and became man, suffered, and rose on the third day, ascended into the heavens, and is coming to judge living and dead.

Nicene Creed (DB, 54).

d. Pagan and Jewish Opposition. St. Cyril of Jerusalem, 348–50

[Although not heretics themselves, the pagan and Jewish polemicists exercised a strong influence on the early Christian heretics. In St. Cyril's famous *Catechetical Lectures on the Creed*, the catechumens are given instructions on how to meet their objections against the Savior's birth from a virgin. The pagans are to be "silenced out of their own fables"; the Jews are to be "confronted with their own scriptures."]

28. . . . O you Jews, which is the more difficult, for a virgin to bear a child, or for a rod to be quickened into a living thing? You admit that at the time of Moses a perfectly straight rod took the form of a serpent and became an object of terror to him who cast it down, and he who before had held the rod fast now fled from it as a dragon. . . .

29. These stories are highly suggestive, but the Jews still contradict and are not impressed by the argument drawn from the rod so long as there is no reference to births similar to our case, births which are strange and beyond nature. Ask them, therefore, the following questions: From whom was Eve begotten at the beginning? What mother conceived her who was without mother? Do not the Scriptures say that she was formed from the side of a man? Why cannot a child be born without a father from the womb of a virgin? Woman owed a debt of gratitude to man, for Eve sprang from Adam, conceived by no mother, but brought forth as it were by man alone. Now Mary paid this debt of gratitude when, through the power of God, of herself alone and not by man, immaculately she brought forth by the Holy Spirit.

Catechetical Lectures, 12, 28–29
(PG, 33, 760–61).

e. Apollinarianism. St. Gregory of Nazianzus, 382

[Apollinaris, a vigorous opponent of Arianism, to emphasize Christ's divinity, denied His full manhood, holding that the Word, the second Person of the Trinity,

took the place of the human soul of Christ. Apollinarianism was condemned at the First Council of Constantinople (381) and a year later at a synod of Rome under
Pope Damasus. In the anathemas of St. Gregory we have
a compendious statement of the heresies directed against
Christ and His Mother.]

If anyone does not accept holy Mary as Mother of
God, he is cut off from the Deity.

If anyone should say that Christ passed through the
Virgin as through a channel, and was not fashioned in
a way that is divine as well as human . . . he is
equally godless.

If anyone should say that the man was fashioned
and only afterwards did God steal in, he also is to be
condemned. . . .

If anyone introduces two Sons, one of God the
Father, the other of the Mother, and not one and the
same Son, may he forfeit his share in the adoption. . . .

Letter 101 (PG, 37, 177–180).

f. Nestorianism. The Council of Ephesus, 431

[Nestorius became Patriarch of Constantinople in 428.
Faced with the great Christological problem—explaining
the union of the divine with the human nature in Christ—
Nestorius reduced the union to one of the moral order
by asserting that God the Word and Jesus were two dis-
tinct persons, two individuals united in the moral person
called Christ. Nestorius' heterodoxy was unmasked when
one of his priests openly preached that Mary was not the
Mother of God but merely the mother of the man Christ.
Accordingly, Mary may be called *Christotokos* (Christ-
bearer), but not *Theotokos* (God-bearer or Mother of

God [1]). The most vigorous opponent of Nestorius was St. Cyril of Alexandria. Cyril's second letter to Nestorius (430), in which he defends the propriety of referring to the holy Virgin as Theotokos, was read and approved at the Council of Ephesus (the third ecumenical council, 431). The famous anathemas of Cyril, although probably never read at Ephesus, were regarded by the Second Council of Constantinople (the fifth ecumenical council, 553) as part of the actual proceedings of Ephesus (see DB, 113, note 2). An excerpt from Cyril's letter and the first of his twelve anathemas are given below.]

Nor do we say that the nature of the Word became flesh by undergoing change, nor that it was transformed into an entire man of soul and body; rather do we say that the Word, in a manner indescribable and incomprehensible, personally (hypostatically) united to Himself flesh animated by a rational soul, and thus became Man and was called the Son of Man. . . .

Nor was He first born of the holy Virgin as an ordinary man, in such a way that the Word only afterwards descended upon Him; rather was He united [with flesh] in the womb itself, and thus is said to have undergone birth according to the flesh, inasmuch as He makes His own the birth of His own flesh. . . . For this reason [the holy Fathers] have boldly proclaimed the holy Virgin Theotokos.

Second Letter to Nestorius (DB, 111a).

---

[1] The suffix *tokos*, from the verb *tikto*, means more than "bearer." It includes the whole process of motherhood: conception, gestation and birth. Hence *Theotokos* is best translated "Mother of God."

Anathema 1. If anyone does not confess that Emmanuel is in truth God, and that the holy Virgin is, in consequence, Theotokos (Mother of God), since she brought forth according to the flesh the Word of God who has become flesh, let him be anathema.

Appended to the *Fourth Letter to Nestorius* (DB, 113).

PART II

THE EARLIEST ENCOMIUMS TO MARY

★

[Creeds and anathemas are necessary to fix the faith in the minds of Christians. But they give only an inadequate portrait of God, of Christ, and of His Mother. They tell us little of the warmth and devotion that pervaded the hearts of those who believed; little of that vital assimilation of the mysteries of the faith in which future dogmas are already latent and which only await authentic expression. Thus the whole of Mariology, the truths of Mary's motherhood, her virginity, her mediation, her sinlessness, the incorruptibility of her body, are foreshadowed in a tendency from the beginning to associate Mary, the second Eve, with Christ, the second Adam. It is this theme that is developed with ever-unfolding variations in what may be called the Church's symphonic hymn to Mary. The theme is stated in the writings of the early Christian apologetes and reaches an early climax in the hymns of St. Ephrem, Mary's first poet.]

1. THE EARLY CHRISTIAN APOLOGETES

a. Mary, the Second Eve. St. Justin Martyr, c. 155

The First-born of the Father is born of the Virgin, in order that the disobedience caused by the serpent might be destroyed in the same manner in which it had originated. For Eve, an undefiled virgin, conceived the word of the serpent, and brought forth disobedience and death. But the Virgin Mary, filled with faith and joy, when the angel Gabriel announced to her the good tidings that the Spirit of the Lord would come upon her, and the power of the Highest would over-shadow her, and therefore the Holy One born of her would be the Son of God, answered: "Be it done unto me according to thy word" (Lk. 1:35). And, indeed, she gave birth to Him, concerning whom we have shown so many passages of Scripture were written, and by whom God destroys both the serpent and those angels and men who have become like the serpent, but frees from death those who repent of their sins and believe in Christ.

Dialogue with Trypho, 100 (PG, 6, 709–712; tr. T. B. Falls, FC, *St. Justin Martyr* [New York, 1948], pp. 304–305).

b. Mary, Eve's Advocate. St. Irenaeus, c. 177

For as Eve was seduced by the word of an angel to avoid God after she had disobeyed His word, so Mary, by the word of an angel, had the glad tidings delivered to her that she might bear God, obeying His word. And whereas the former had disobeyed God, yet the latter was persuaded to obey God in order that the Virgin Mary might be the advocate of the virgin Eve. And as the human race was sentenced to death by means of a virgin, it is set aright by means of a virgin. The balance is restored to equilibrium: a virgin's dis-obedience is saved by a virgin's obedience. For while the sin of the first man was emended by the correction of the First-born, the guile of the serpent was overcome by the simplicity of the dove [Mary], and we were set free from those chains by which we had been bound to death.

Against Heresies, 5, 19, 1 (Harvey, 2, 376; PG, 7, 1175–76).

c. Salvation through the Second Eve. Tertullian, c. 210

For into Eve, as yet a virgin, had crept the devil's word, the framer of death. Equally, into a virgin was to be introduced God's Word, the builder of life; so that what had been lost through one sex might by the same sex be restored and saved. Eve had believed the serpent, Mary believed Gabriel. The fault which the one committed by believing, by believing the other emended. "But Eve at that moment conceived nothing in her womb from the devil's word!" Ah, but she did conceive. For her the word of the devil was seed, that she might from that time forth give birth as an outcast, in sorrow give birth. As a consequence, she gave birth to a devil, his brother's murderer. Mary, on the contrary, bore Him who was one day to save Israel, His own brother according to the flesh, His murderer. God, therefore, sent down into the Virgin's womb His Word, our good Brother, to blot out the memory of that evil brother.

On the Flesh of Christ, 17 (CSEL, 70, 233).

d. Mary's Incorruptibility. St. Hippolytus, d. 235

[The Ark of the Covenant, as type and figure of Christ, leads Hippolytus to associate the sinlessness of Christ with that of His Mother, a characteristic form in which the Immaculate Conception is expressed in the early Church. The passage will be used as well to witness to the incorruptibility of Mary's body, the basis for the dogma of the Assumption.]

The ark which was made of incorruptible timber (Ex. 15:10) was the Savior. The ark symbolized the tabernacle of His body, which was impervious to decay and engendered no sinful corruption. . . . The Lord was sinless, because, in His humanity, He was fashioned out of incorruptible wood, that is, out of the Virgin and the Holy Ghost, lined within and without as with the purest gold of the Word of God.

Fragment quoted by Theodoret,
Dialogue, 1 (PG, 10, 864-65).

2. Mary's First Poet: St. Ephrem the Syrian, d. 373

[*Ephrem* in the Hebrew means "fruitful," and out of the abundance of this great liturgical poet's heart have flowed the richest encomiums to Mary in the early Church. The rhythms of Ephrem deal with many mysteries of the faith; but, to quote Benedict XV, who raised St. Ephrem to the dignity of Doctor of the Universal Church, "This Harp of the Holy Spirit never sings sweeter songs than when he has set his strings to sing the praises of Mary" (AAS, 12, 1920, 467). In the selections given, St. Ephrem captures something of the original wonder of Mary's motherhood, her giving birth as a virgin, her role of mediation and her absolute sinlessness. The recurrent theme is Mary, the second Eve.]

a. The Virgin Mother of God

1. Awake, O my harp, thy chords, in praise of Mary the Virgin. Lift up thy voice, and sing the generation utterly marvelous of this Virgin, David's daughter, who hath brought forth life to the world.

2. The lover with admiration wonders at her; whilst the curious searcher is suffused with shame and his ear is stopped up, lest he should dare to pry into the Mother who brought forth in virginity inviolate. . . .

12. In Mary's womb became an infant He who from eternity is equal to the Father. He gave us part in His own greatness, and Himself made acquisition of our weakness. Mortal was He made along with us, that by infusing into us His life, we might die no more.

16. Mary is the garden upon which descended from the Father the rain of benedictions. From that rain she herself sprinkled the face of Adam. Whereupon he returned to life, and arose from the sepulchre—he who had been buried by his foes in hell.

20. Lo, a virgin is become a mother, preserving virginity with its seals unbroken. . . . She is made God's Mother and is at the same time a servant, and the work of His wisdom.

21. The Virgin, who gave birth to the Only-begotten, has nurtured God and Man, has become

Mother of the hidden Little One, who of the Father was born perfect and is made an Infant in her womb.

24. In Eden Eve became a debtor, and the debt whereby her posterity in their generation were doomed to death was written in letters large. The Serpent, that wicked scrivener, wrote it out, signed and gave it force with the seal of his fraud.

26. Eve was a debtor to sin. But for Mary the debt was reserved that the daughter might pay her mother's debts and tear up the handwriting that had handed on her mother's tears as a legacy to all generations.

27. Mary carried Fire in her hands and embraced Flame with her arms. To the Flame she gave her breasts to suck, to the Nourisher of all she gave of her milk. Who can possibly tell of her?

30. Since Mary was the Virgin inviolate—prefigured by the blest land of Eden before its surface was torn by furrows—there blossomed from her bosom the Tree of Life, the taste of which . . . gives life to souls.

45. Let the word of life be sent by Thy Majesty to the dwelling place of the dead, and say to Eve lying in the sepulchre: "Thy daughter, with virginity unimpaired, has brought forth the Child who will pay thy debt."

51. Blessed art thou, Mary, daughter of David; and blessed is the Fruit which thou hast given us. Blessed the Father who sent His Son for our salvation, and

blessed the Spirit Advocate who has taught us her mystery. Blessed be His Name.

Hymns on Blessed Mary, 18 (Lamy, 2, 605–619;
tr. based on Livius, pp. 427 ff.).

b. A Mother's Song to Her Son

1. With wonder have I contemplated Mary suckling the Nourisher of the tribes, who is become an Infant. In a maiden's womb dwelt He who fills the world.

5. As she nursed the Child, she caressed Him, fondled and petted Him with coaxing words; and then adored Him, saying: "Bid me, my Master, embrace Thee.

6. "Since my Son Thou art, with my nursery rhymes [lullabies] will I soothe Thee. And, for all that I am Thy Mother, I shall honor Thee. My Son, to whom I have given birth, older than me Thou art. My Lord, though I carried Thee, it is Thou that upholdest me.

9. "Lo, whole Thou art with me, and whole art Thou hidden in Thy Father. All heights of the heaven are full of Thy Majesty, and yet my bosom is not too straitened for Thee.

11. "Let heaven hold me in its embraces; for above it I am honored. For heaven, in truth, was not Thy Mother, but Thou madest it Thy throne.

12. "How much more honorable and venerable is the King's mother than His throne. I will give Thee thanks, O Lord, because Thou hast willed me to be

Thy Mother. In gentle hymns will I celebrate Thy praise.

19. "Let Eve, our first mother, now hear and come to me. Let her lift up her head that was bent low under the garden's shame.

20. "Let her uncover her face and give Thee thanks, because Thou hast taken away her confusion. Let her hear the voice of perfect peace, because her daughter has paid her debt.

21. "The Serpent, her seducer, has been crushed by Thee, the Shoot that is sprung from my bosom. By Thee the Cherubim and the sword have been taken away, that Adam might return to the paradise whence he was driven out."

Hymns on Blessed Mary, 19 (Lamy, 2, 621–25; tr. Livius, pp. 430 ff.).

c. On the Annunciation

[This is the last in Lamy's collection of St. Ephrem's hymns on the Virgin. Remarkable throughout for its doctrinal content, in verses 29–30 it gives eloquent expression to the belief that Mary was never under Satan's domination, the basis for the later dogmatic declarations that Mary was preserved from original sin and from that "return to dust," which marked the penalty of Adam's sin.]

1. Eve wrote in Eden the great handwriting of debt whereby her posterity should pass on death to all generations; the Serpent signed the fatal book, sealed and secured it with the signet of fraud.

3. Eve brought on the sin, and the debt was reserved for the Virgin Mary, that she might pay the debts of her mother, and tear up the handwriting under which were groaning all generations.

8. Winging his downward flight the Angel came to Mary, adored her and brought her the tidings. . . .

11. "Peace with thee, daughter of men, because thou hast been chosen by God for spouse, that still preserving thy virginity, thou mayest be Mother of His Beloved One, and bring forth the Ancient of days who will raise up again the ruins of the world."

13. Mary said: "How without man shall generation be given? A child thou announcest to me, show me His father: a virgin intact I am, nor ever know I man.

14. "The field that ne'er was sown how shall it see its produce? To me thou announcest fruit. Who is the husbandman? How without seed may I see the yield of fruit?"

15. The angel answered: "Be silent, Mary. Thy husbandman needs no seed: Himself coming down will sow Himself in thy womb, from thee will He spring up as the herb, and will satiate the world's hunger.

17. "The Holy Ghost is with thee. He it is who will foster and sanctify thy womb, and the power of the Most High will come down to overshadow thee, and from thee shall go forth the Infant who will crush the Serpent's head."

19. The Maiden said to the Angel, "Behold, here I am, the handmaid of the Lord; the Creator can dwell

in His creature, and fitting is it that the Workman according to His mercy should visit the work of His hands."

20. The Serpent and Eve dug a grave and thrust the guilty Adam down into hell: but Gabriel came and spoke with Mary, and thereupon was laid open the mystery whereby all the dead are again raised up.

21. Adam's virgin entertained the Liar, by whom she was deceived; most perversely she hearkened to him, foolishly believed, and made Adam naked through the garden's bitter fruit.

22. Then arose Mary, the daughter of David, who obtained peace from the Angel, wove a garment of glory, gave her vestment to cover the nakedness of Adam; whilst the Spouse in His beauty stood by in His bride chamber.

23. Two virgins there were, but of these two very different was the conduct: the one laid prostrate her husband, the other uplifted her father. Through Eve man found his grave, through Mary he was called to heaven.

27. On the branch of the Virgin Mary, God, coming down from on high, hung the fruit, of which in Eden they had not tasted [of the Tree of Life]; from Mary they plucked it, because the Fruit that gives strength to its eaters, out of love descended upon them.

29. Concupiscence and pride were lurking in the tree of knowledge: the Virgin conceived fruit without concupiscence, that the deadly concupiscence of

the human race might through her forever be done away.

30. God's Eden is Mary; in her is no tree of knowledge [experience of good and evil], no serpent that harms, no Eve that kills, but from her springs the Tree of Life that restores the exiles to Eden.

31. The Tree of Life which the Cherub and flaming sword are keeping, lo, now has its place in the Virgin most pure, whom Joseph is guarding. The Jews with reproaches persecute the Maiden, supposing, as they do, Joseph to be father of this Tree.

32. The guard has laid aside his sword, because the Fruit that he guarded has been sent from on high to earth for the fallen. Mortals ate of it and thereby acquired life. Blessed is the Fruit that Mary brought forth.

On the Annunciation of the Mother of God, Hymn 3
(Lamy, 3, 979–989; tr. Livius, 437 ff.).

d. Mary's Sinlessness

[In the following two brief excerpts, the purity and the spotlessness of Mary find their exemplar in the Father and the Son.]

The Word of the Father came forth from His Bosom, and in another bosom He put on a body. From a Bosom He came forth to a bosom. These pure Bosoms were filled with Him. Blessed is He who dwells in us.

Hymn on the Resurrection of Christ, 7
(Lamy, 2, 743; tr. Livius, p. 435).

Thou and Thy Mother are the only ones who are perfectly beautiful in every respect; for there is no spot in Thee, O Lord, nor any taint in Thy Mother.

The Nisibis Hymn, 27 (G. Bickell
[Leipzig, 1886], p. 122).

e. Mary's Virginity and the Virgin Birth

[The original commentary of Ephrem on the *Diatesseron* of Tatian (c. 165) remains only in fragments. The following extract is taken from the Latin reconstruction of Mösinger (Venice, 1876), pp. 23–24, as reproduced by J. Rendel Harris in *Fragments of the Commentary of Ephrem Syrus upon the Diatesseron* (London, 1895), pp. 31–32.]

And yet how could it be that she, who was the dwelling and habitation of the Spirit and whom the power of God overshadowed, should afterwards become the wife of a mortal man, and in conformity with the primeval curse bring forth in pain? For since Mary is blessed among women, through her was revoked that original malediction by which children are born in pain and accursed. But just as the Lord entered the Cenacle although the doors were closed, so in the same way did He come forth from the virginal womb. For this Virgin, without experiencing the pains of childbirth, really and truly gave birth. If, moreover, the fact that certain disciples were called the brothers of the Lord should lead some to believe that they were the sons of Mary, let them know that even Christ Himself was called the son of Joseph, and this not only by the Jews, but by His mother Mary herself.

PART III

THE TRADITION OF THE WEST

★

[Less disturbed by the early heresies, which had their origins for the most part in the East, the great Latin Fathers are more incidental in their encomiums to Mary. Nestorius never claimed any adherents in the West, and, therefore, did not evoke that immediate devotional reaction which will be found to mark the development of Mariology in the East (see below, p. 49). The principal emphasis in the West is on the defense of the perpetual virginity of the Mother of God, a truth of particular relevance where a life of celibacy was obligatory for the clergy as early as the year 385, and where, as in the East, the state of virginity had long been upheld as the crowning ideal of Christian womanhood. Other aspects of Mary's fulness of grace, and in particular her grace of sinlessness, are not ignored.]

1. MARY EVER VIRGIN

a. The "Brethren" of the Lord. St. Jerome, c. 383

[With the exception of Tertullian after his Montanist defection, no Christian writer of any renown had ever questioned the perpetual virginity of the Mother of God. The references to the "brethren" of the Lord which recur from time to time in the gospel narrative were understood to refer either to the sons of Joseph by a previous

24

marriage or to the Lord's cousins or kinsmen. In a letter against Helvidius, who is known only for his lack of reverence towards the Virgin, St. Jerome defends not only the perpetual virginity of Mary but that of Joseph as well. To prove that the "brethren" of the Lord could not have been the children of Mary, Jerome's basic appeal is to Christian tradition, an argument no less convincing for all that it is couched in language that may offend those who regard temperance in debate as more desirable than the truth which results.]

18. [16] There are things which, in your extreme ignorance, you Helvidius had never read, and therefore you neglected the whole range of Scripture and employed your madness in outraging the Virgin, like the man in the story who being unknown to everybody and finding that he could devise no good deed by which to gain renown, burned the temple of Diana: and when no one revealed the sacrilegious act, it is said that he himself went up and down proclaiming that he was the man who had applied the fire. The rulers of Ephesus were curious to know what made him do this thing, whereupon he replied that if he could not have fame for good deeds, all men should give him credit for bad ones. Grecian history relates the incident. But you do worse. You have set on fire the temple of the Lord's body, you have defiled the sanctuary of the Holy Spirit from which you are determined to make a team of four brethren and a heap of sisters come forth. In a word, joining in the chorus of the Jews you say, "Is not this the carpenter's son?

is not his mother called Mary? and his brethren James
and Joseph and Simon and Judas? and his sisters, are
they not all with us? The word *all* would not be used
if there were not a crowd of them." Pray tell me, who
before you appeared, was acquainted with this blas-.
phemy? Who thought the theory worth two-pence?
You have gained your desire and have become notor-
ious by crime. . . .

19. [17] . . . Feeling himself to be a smatterer, he,
Helvidius, produces Tertullian as a witness and quotes
the words of Victorinus bishop of Petavium. Of Tertullian I say no more than that he did not belong to
the Church. But as regards Victorinus, I assert what
has already been proved from the gospel—that he
spoke of the brethren of the Lord not as being sons of
Mary, but brethren in the sense I have explained, that
is to say, brethren in point of kinship not by nature.
We are, however, spending our strength on trifles,
and, leaving the fountain of truth, are following the
tiny streams of opinion. Might I not array against you
the whole series of ancient writers? Ignatius, Polycarp,
Irenaeus, Justin Martyr, and many other apostolic and
eloquent men, who against Ebion, Theodotus of By-
zantium, and Valentinus, held these same views, and
wrote volumes replete with wisdom. If you had ever
read what they wrote, you would be a wiser man. . . .

21. [19] . . . You say that Mary did not continue
a virgin: I claim still more, that Joseph himself on
account of Mary was a virgin, so that from a virgin
wedlock a virgin son was born. For if as a holy man

he does not come under the imputation of fornication, and it is nowhere written that he had another wife, but was the guardian of Mary (whom he was supposed to have to wife) rather than her husband, the conclusion is that he who was thought worthy to be called the father of the Lord, remained a virgin.

The Perpetual Virginity of Blessed Mary, Against Helvidius
(PL, 23, 209 ff.; tr. W. H. Fremantle, NPN, 6, 343 f.).

b. Special Patroness of Virgins. St. Ambrose, 391–92

Oh, the riches of Mary's virginity. . . . As a cloud she waters the earth with the rain of Christ's grace. For it has been written of her: "Lo, the Lord cometh seated upon a light cloud" (Isa. 19:1) . . . so light indeed as to lighten and to free this world from its heavy burden of sin. She was indeed light who carried in her womb the Remission of sins. She it was who lightened and raised John formed in the womb of his mother—John, who, an infant, at the sound of her voice leaped for joy. . . . Receive, then, receive, O consecrated virgins, the spiritual rain that falls from this cloud, which will temper the burning desires of the body. Receive this rain to control all passion of body and bring cool refreshment to the interior of your soul. It is the rain from this consecrated cloud that our fathers announced to us as the world's future salvation. . . . Run after this good cloud, for within her she has brought forth a fountain to water the face of the earth. . . . Prepare yourselves as vessels of the Lord that you may receive this fountain of living water, the source of virginity, the healing balm of integrity, the perfume of faith and the sweet flowering of gracious mercy. . . ."

The Instruction of a Virgin, 13, 81–86 (PL, 16, 325–26).

c. Mary's Perpetual Virginity. Pope St. Siricius, 392

Surely we cannot deny that Your Reverence was perfectly justified in rebuking him on the score of Mary's children, and that you had good reason to be horrified at the thought that another birth might issue from the same virginal womb from which Christ was born according to the flesh. For the Lord Jesus would never have chosen to be born of a virgin if he had ever judged that she would be so incontinent as to contaminate with the seed of human intercourse the birthplace of the Lord's body, that court of the Eternal King. To assert such a view is to do nothing less than to accept as a basis that Jewish falsehood which holds that He could not have been born of a virgin. And once the weight of episcopal authority is gained for the view that Mary gave issue to many children, they will strive with even greater zeal to attack the truth of [Christian] faith.

Letter to Anysisus, Bishop of Thessalonica
(Mansi, 3, 675; DB, 91).

d. The Virgin Birth. St. Jerome, d. 419

Christ is a virgin, and the Mother of our Virgin is herself ever a virgin; she is Mother and Virgin. Although the doors were shut, Jesus entered within;

in the sepulchre that was Mary, which was new and hewn in hardest rock, no one either before or afterwards was laid. She is a "garden enclosed, a fountain sealed" (Cant. 4:12). . . . She is the Eastern gate, whereof Ezechiel speaks, always shut and full of light, which closing on itself brings forth from itself the Holy of Holies; whereby the Sun of Justice, and our High Priest, according to the order of Melchisedech, enters in and goes out. Let them tell me how Jesus entered [the Cenacle] when the doors were shut . . . and I will tell them how holy Mary is both Mother and Virgin, Virgin after childbirth, and Mother before she was married.

To Pammachius, Letter 49 [48], 21 (CSEL, 54, 386).

e. *Virginity and Virgin Birth. The Tome of Pope St. Leo I, 449*

[Eutyches, a monk of Alexandria, had allowed his anti-Nestorian zeal to betray him into the conclusion that the divine and the human natures were so perfectly blended in Christ as to result in a single nature (*mono—phusis*, whence the term *Monophysite*). At the Fourth Ecumenical Council of Chalcedon (451), in which the Monophysites were condemned, Leo's letter to the Emperor Flavian against Eutyches was read and Leo himself acclaimed in the historic words: "Peter has spoken through Leo" (see DB, 143, and note 3). A section of this letter is cited for its doctrinal pronouncement on the perpetual virginity of the Mother of God, which includes as well the virgin birth.]

He [Eutyches] did not realize what he was bound to hold on the Incarnation of the Word of God. Nor was he willing to seek the light of understanding through a diligent search of the wide range of the Sacred Scriptures. And yet, he might have listened attentively to that common and universal confession in which the whole body of the faithful acknowledges its belief in God the Father Almighty, and in Jesus Christ, His only-begotten Son our Lord, who was born of the Holy Ghost and the Virgin Mary. By these three statements, the devices of almost all heretics are overthrown. . . . Unquestionably, therefore, He was conceived of the Holy Spirit within the womb of His Virgin Mother. She brought Him forth without the loss of virginity, even as she conceived Him without its loss. . . . That birth, so wondrously unique and so uniquely wonderful, must not be understood in such a way that the distinctive properties of His humanity were excluded through this newness of His creation. For while it is true that the Holy Spirit gave fruitfulness to the Virgin, yet the reality of His body was received from her body; and "Wisdom building itself a house" (Prov. 9:11), "the Word became flesh and dwelt among us" (Jn. 1:14)—that is, in that flesh which He took from man and which He quickened with the breath of a higher life. . . .

The Son of God, therefore, came down from His heavenly throne without relinquishing the glory of His Father, and entered this lower world by way of a new order and a new mode of birth. . . . By way of a new mode of birth, insofar as virginity inviolate which knew not the desire of the flesh supplied the material of flesh. From His Mother the Lord took nature, not sin. Jesus Christ was born from a virgin's womb, by a miraculous birth. And yet His nature is not on that account unlike to ours, for He that is true God is also true Man.

Letter 28 to Emperor Flavian (PL, 54, 763 ff.;
excerpt in DB, 143 f.).

f. The First Lateran Council. Pope St. Martin I, 649

[The last of the great Christological heresies was that of Monothelitism. The Monothelites held that there was but a single will (*mono–thelema*) in Christ, and that the divine, to the exclusion of His human, will. They were first condemned at a local council held at the Lateran Palace under the auspices of Pope St. Martin I (649), and again at the Sixth Ecumenical Council of Constantinople (the third to be held there, 681). At this ecumenical gathering the canons of the Lateran Council were received and an accompanying letter of Pope St. Agatho, Martin's successor, was read. Once again the position of the Roman See is acknowledged in the acclamation of the assembled Fathers: "Peter has spoken through Agatho" (see DB, p. 121, note 1; p. 134, note 2). The third of the twenty canons drawn up at the Lateran and forwarded to Constantinople is given below.]

Canon 3. If anyone does not in accord with the Holy Fathers acknowledge the holy and ever virgin and immaculate Mary as really and truly the Mother of God, inasmuch as she, in the fulness of time, and without seed, conceived by the Holy Spirit God the Word Himself, who before all time was born of God the Father, and without loss of integrity brought Him forth, and after His birth preserved her virginity inviolate, let him be condemned.

The Lateran Council, can. 3 (Mansi, 10, 1151; DB, 256).

2. MARY'S FULNESS OF GRACE

a. *"Hail, Full of Grace."* St. Augustine, d. 430

What art thou, Mary, thou who wilt presently bring forth? Whence hast thou merited, whence hast thou obtained this favor? Whence is it that He who made thee will be made in thee? Whence, I say, does this great gift come to thee? Thou art a virgin, thou art holy, thou hast vowed a vow. True, thou hast merited much; or better, thou hast received much. But how hast thou merited it? He who made thee is being made in thee. He is made in thee by whom thou thyself wast made; rather should I say, by whom heaven and earth were made, by whom all things were made; the Word of God is made flesh in thee, by taking flesh, not by losing divinity. The Word is joined to flesh; the Word is wedded to flesh, and the bridal chamber of this exalted marriage is thy womb. Let me repeat, the bridal chamber of this exalted marriage between the Word and flesh is thy womb, whence "he, the bridegroom, goes forth from his bridal chamber" (Ps. 18:6). He finds thee a virgin at His conception. He leaves thee a virgin at His birth.

He gives thee fecundity. He takes not away thy integrity. Whence is this to thee? Perhaps I am too forward in asking such questions of a virgin and, I might say, somewhat rude in shocking thy bashfulness with such words. But I see a virgin who is indeed bashful, and yet one who can answer and at the same time put me in my place. "Dost thou ask of me whence is this? I blush to answer thy questions as to my blessedness. Rather, listen to the Angel's salutation. . . . Believe him whom I believed. Do you ask whence have I this favor? Let the Angel reply." Tell me, Angel, whence has Mary this? "I already said when I saluted her: 'Hail, full of grace.'"

Sermon 291, On the Birthday of John the Baptist,
5, 6 (PL, 38, 1319).

b. Mary's Grace of Sinlessness. St. Augustine, 415

[Pelagius, in an effort to bolster his denial of original sin and man's need of grace in order to live a life of sinlessness, appeals to the saints of the Old Law, who were apparently sinless. In handling this difficulty, Augustine deals only with the question of personal sin. With regard to Mary, however, he delivers a verdict which is universal enough to exclude sin of any kind.]

Now with the exception of the holy Virgin Mary in regard to whom, out of respect for the Lord, I do not propose to have a single question raised on the subject of sin—after all, how do we know what greater degree of grace for a complete victory over sin was conferred on her who merited to conceive and bring forth Him who all admit was without sin—to repeat then: with the exception of this Virgin, if we could bring together into one place all those holy men and women, while they lived here, and ask them whether they were without sin, what are we to suppose that they would have replied? Would it be the reply of this man [Pelagius] or that of John the Apostle? I ask you. No matter how they excelled in holiness during their stay in this body, if they could have been asked, they would have exclaimed with one voice: "If we say that we have no sin, we deceive ourselves, and the truth is not in us."

On Nature and Grace, 36 [42] (CSEL, 60, 263–64).

3. MARY, THE MOTHER OF GOD

[The Lerins, two islands lying in the Bay of Cannes, were renowned in the fifth century as the center of Western theological learning. St. Vincent, priest of the monastery, there composed his famous commonitory or memorandum, *On the Antiquity and Universality of the Catholic Faith Against the Profane Novelties of All Heretics*. Since these novelties centered for the most part on a denial of either the humanity or the divinity of Christ, it is not surprising that Vincent should devote a whole chapter to the dogma of Mary's divine motherhood, proclaimed only three years before at the Council of Ephesus. Before citing this chapter we shall sum up in Vincent's own words the basic Christological heresies which implicitly denied Mary's privilege as Mother of God.]

a. The Christological Heresies, a Summary. St. Vincent of Lerins, 434

First, then, the doctrine of Photinus. According to him, God is singular and unique, and one has to conceive of Him in the manner of the Jews. He denies the plenitude of the Trinity and denies that there is either the Person of the Word or the Person of the Holy Spirit. As for Christ, he asserts that, though unique, He is merely a human being, and ascribes His origin to Mary. He states dogmatically that we must show reverence only to the Person of God the Father, but to Christ only as a man. Thus Photinus.

Apollinaris boasts of consenting to the doctrine of the Unity of the Trinity—though not in the full purity of the faith. But he blasphemes openly with regard to the Incarnation of our Lord. He says that there was no human soul in the body of our Savior, or, if there were one, that it had neither mind nor reason. He asserts that the flesh of our Lord was not formed from the flesh of Holy Virgin Mary, but descended from Heaven into the Virgin, and he taught, in constant wavering and doubt, sometimes that she was co-eternal with God the Word, sometimes that she was only created out of the divinity of the Word. He refused to admit two substances in Christ—one divine, the other human; one from the Father, the other from the mother. He believed that the Word's nature was itself divided, as though the one remained in God and the other had been converted into flesh. Whereas the

Truth says that the One Christ consists of two substances, he—contrary to truth—asserts that from One
Divinity of Christ two substances were made. This is
the doctrine of Apollinaris.

Nestorius, who suffered from a disease quite contrary to that of Apollinaris, suddenly introduces two
persons while pretending to distinguish two substances
in Christ. In his unheard-of wickedness he assumes
that there are two sons of God, two Christs—the one
God, the other man; one, begotten of the Father, the
other, of the mother. Thus he asserts that Holy Mary
is not to be called *"Theotokos"* but *"Christotokos,"*
since she gave birth not to Christ-God, but Christ-
man. But if one believes that he speaks in his writings
of *one* Christ and that he teaches *one* Person of
Christ, let him be careful not to give too easy credence
to such an interpretation. Nestorius contrives this
wording skillfully to deceive his readers—in order to
recommend evil doctrines more easily through the in-
termediary of good ones, according to the words of
the Apostle: "was that then which is good, made death
unto me?" (Rom. 7:13). Well, either he deceitfully
overemphasizes in certain passages of his writings that
he believes in *one* Christ and *one* Person of Christ, or
he pretends that, only after the birth from the Virgin,
both Persons were united in *one* Christ. But this statement is made in such a way that it means that at the
time of the Virgin's conception or bearing, and even
for some time after, two Christs existed. Thus, though
Christ, as merely man, was born the first, and unique,

and not joined in Unity of Person to the Word of God, afterwards the Person of the Word descended into Him, assuming Him. Although now, having been assumed (by the Word), He abides in the glory of God, yet it would seem that for a time there was no difference between Him and other men.

The Commonitories, ch. 12 (ed. G. Rauschen, *Florilegium Patristicum*, fasc. 5 [Bonnae, 1906], tr. by Rudolph E. Morris in FC, 7, 288–290).

b. Theotokos, an Explanation of the Dogma

Thus, this unity of the Person in Christ was formed and completed, not after the birth from the Virgin, but in the very womb of the Virgin. We must therefore take utmost care to be precise in our confession, so as to say that Christ is not merely *one*, but that He always has been *one*. It were, indeed, an intolerable blasphemy to assert that, although you admit His now being One, you contend that He once was not One but Two—One after His baptism, but Two at the time of His birth. We cannot escape this enormous sacrilege unless we assert that humanity has been united to divinity through the unity of Person, not through the ascension or resurrection or baptism, but within the Mother, in her womb, and—even more—in the Virginal Conception itself. Because of this Unity of Person, it happens that what is proper to God is ascribed to the man, and what is proper to the flesh is ascribed to God—indifferently and without distinction. Therefore, as it is written in Holy Scripture: "He that

D

descended from heaven, the Son of man who is in heaven" (Jn. 3:13), and "crucified the Lord of glory" (I Cor. 2:8) on earth. Furthermore, since the body of the Lord was made and created, it is said that the "Word" of God Himself was "made" (Jn. 1:14), His wisdom filled up (Eccli. 24:35), His knowledge created (Eccli. 1:4; 24:36); therefore do the prophetic writings refer to His hands and feet as "pierced" (Ps. 21:17). Through this Unity of Person it also becomes perfectly clear—by reason of a similar mystery—that it is most truly Catholic to believe (and most impious to deny) that the Word of God Himself was born from the Virgin even as the flesh of the Word was born from an Immaculate Mother.

Therefore, may God forbid that anyone should attempt to defraud Holy Mary of her privileges of divine grace and her special glory. For by a unique favor of our Lord and God she is confessed to be the most true and most blessed Mother of God (theotokos). She is truly the Mother of God, not merely in name, as a certain impious heresy claims, because she gave birth to a man who later became God, as we call the mother of priests or bishops such, because she gave birth, not to a priest or a bishop, but to a child who later became one. Not thus, I say, is Holy Mary the Mother of God, but rather because, as has already been said, in her sacred womb was accomplished the mystery that, by reason of a certain singular and unique Unity of Person, even as the Word is flesh in flesh, so the man is God in God.

Ibid., ch. 15 (tr. in FC, 7, 295–296).

4. MARY, THE MOTHER OF MEN

a. Mary's Mystical Motherhood. St. Peter Chrysologus d. 450

Mary is called Mother. And when is Mary not a mother? "The gathering together of the waters he called seas (*maria*)" (Gen. 1:10). Was it not she who conceived in her single womb the people going out from Egypt, that it might come forth a heavenly progeny reborn to a new creation, according to the words of the Apostle: "Our fathers were all under the cloud, and all passed through the sea. And all in Moses were baptised, in the cloud, and in the sea" (Exod. 15:20–21)? That Mary might always lead the way in man's salvation, in her own right, she went with a canticle before that same people, whom the generating waters had brought forth to light. . . . This is a name [Mary] that is kin to prophecy, salutary to the reborn, the hallmark of virginity, the adornment of modesty, the sign of chastity, a sacrifice to God, the virtue of hospitality, fellowship in holiness. With reason, then, is this maternal name that of Christ's Mother. We have said why the Mother is a bride, why Joseph is a spouse, why Mary has the maternal name, to show that everything about the birth of Christ has a mystical significance.

Sermon 146, On the Generation of Christ, 2 (PL, 52, 593).

b. Mary, Mother of the Church. St. Gregory the Great, d. 604

God the Father arranged the nuptials for God His

Son, when, in the womb of the Virgin, He united
Him to human nature, when He willed that He who
was God before all the ages should at the end of the
ages become Man. However, a nuptial union is usually
formed by two persons . . . but we shun as utterly
impious the belief that He is composed of two persons.
Therefore, with greater freedom and assurance, we
may say that these are the nuptials that the Father
arranged for His royal Son: through the mystery of
the Incarnation, He united the holy Church to Him.
Now the bridal chamber of this Bridegroom was the
womb of the Virgin Mother. That is why the Psalmist
says: "He hath set his tabernacle in the sun: and he,
as a bridegroom coming out of his bridal chamber"
(Ps. 18:6). And it was as a bridegroom in fact that he
came forth from His bridal chamber, because to unite
the Church to Himself the Incarnate God went forth
from the inviolate womb of the Virgin.

Homilies on the Gospels, 2, 38, 3 (PL, 76, 1283).

5. CHRIST'S ATTITUDE TOWARD HIS MOTHER

[When one reads for the first time the account of the
marriage feast at Cana and the incident of Mary's inter-
ruption of her Son while He was preaching, he is struck
by a certain tone of coldness and even harshness on the
part of Christ. It is only in the light of the Church's long
tradition on the absolute sinlessness of Mary that we
begin to understand that Christ's tremendous preoccupation with His "Father's business" is in no sense a re-
pudiation of His Mother or her interests. After all, it is
only in the light of the same tradition that we see in the

following words of Christ a denial neither of His divinity nor of the absolute sinlessness of His humanity: " 'Good Master, what shall I do to gain eternal life?' But Jesus said to him, 'Why dost thou call me good? No one is good but God only' " (Mk. 10:18). Once again, that tremendous preoccupation with the things of God, here the transcendent sanctity of God, creates the impression that Christ is speaking depreciatively of His own sacred humanity. Failure to grasp this principle as it applies to Mary might explain why some Fathers of the East,[2] notably St. John Chrysostom, could see in the narrative of Cana a rebuke administered to Mary that was merited. The principle itself will be given eloquent expression by the Latin Fathers of this period.]

a. *The Marriage Feast at Cana. St. Gaudentius, c. 410*

[Gaudentius, Bishop of Brescia, suggests that the wine for which the hour is not yet come is the wine of the Holy Spirit to be given after the Passion and Resurrection of Jesus. However fanciful the exegesis, it reveals an attitude which refuses to see in the words of Christ a rebuke to His Mother.]

Thereupon, that most blessed one, knowing the pro-

---

[2] Although St. John Chrysostom insists that Mary was the object of her Son's reverence, he does suggest that she was subject to the minor vanities of a mother: "Perhaps, too, she suffered something human, as did also His brethren when they said, 'Show thyself to the world,' wishing to reap glory from the miracle. For this reason as well He answered her somewhat sharply, 'What is it to me and to thee, woman? My hour is not yet come.' But that He had exceeding reverence for His Mother, listen to Luke, who records how He was subject to His parents; and to this same Evangelist John, who shows how He provided for her at the very hour of His crucifixion." *On John, Homily 21* [20], 2 (PG, 59, 129–131).

found mystery of this answer, realized as well that the suggestion that she had just made was neither slighted nor spurned. Rather, she understood that, for the mystical sense implied, her request was for the time mysteriously delayed. Otherwise, she would never have said to the waiters, "Do whatever he tells you" (Jn. 2:5); and unless, full as she was of the Holy Spirit after her divine childbearing, she not only knew the meaning of Christ's answer, but also foresaw the whole course of His making the water wine. For what could be hidden from the Mother of Wisdom, from one who was able to contain God, who was the very temple of such great power?

Sermon 9, On Reading the Gospels, 2 (PL, 20, 901).

St. Augustine, 417

5. Unquestionably there is a mystery here and because of this, He appears not to acknowledge His Mother, from whom as the Bridegroom He came forth, when He says to her, "Woman, what is it to me and to thee? My hour is not yet come" (Jn. 2:4). What is the meaning of this? Did He come to the marriage in order to teach men to treat their mothers with contempt? Why, the man to whose marriage He had come was taking a wife with a view to having children. And surely he wished to be honored by the children that he would beget! Are we then to suppose that Jesus had come to the marriage in order to dishonor His Mother, when marriages are celebrated and wives are married with a view to having children,

whom God commands to honor their parents? Unquestionably, brethren, there is some mystery here. And it is a matter of such importance that some have actually fallen into the error against which the Apostle has forewarned us to be on our guard. "I fear," he said, "lest as the serpent seduced Eve by his subtilty, so your minds should be corrupted and fall from the simplicity that is in Christ" (2 Cor. 11:3). These men set the gospel at naught and assert that Jesus was not born of the Virgin Mary. And to bolster their error, they would try to use this passage by way of support for their statement, "How could she be His Mother, to whom He said, 'Woman, what is it to me and to thee?'"

9. Why, then, does the Son say to His Mother: "What is it to me and to thee; my hour is not yet come"? Our Lord Jesus Christ was both God and Man. Inasmuch as He was God, He had no mother; inasmuch as He was Man, He had. She was, then, the Mother of His flesh, of His humanity, of His weakness which He received for us. The miracle, however, that He was to perform, was to be performed in virtue of His divinity and not in virtue of His infirmity, insofar as He was God and not insofar as He was born in weakness—although the weak things of God are stronger than men (see I Cor. 1:25). . . . Since, then, Mary was not the Mother of His divinity and since the miracle requested would be wrought through His divinity, He answers her: "Woman, what is it to me and to thee?" But do not think that I renounce thee

as My Mother, for the hour is not yet come. There shall I acknowledge thee [as Mother] when that weakness that Thou didst mother shall begin to hang upon the Cross. . . .[3]

On the Gospel of John, Treatise 8 (PL, 35, 1452).

b. Did Christ Disown His Mother? St. Ambrose, c. 387

"My mother and my brethren are they who hear the word of God and keep it" (see Lk. 11:27-28). The Teacher of morals, who sets Himself up as an example to others, and is in fact the preceptor, actually carries out His own precepts. Before enjoining on others that he who leaves not his father and mother is not worthy of the Son of God, He first in His own person subjects Himself to this sentence. Not that He should thereby renounce the duty of filial piety toward His Mother—after all, it is His command: "He who honoreth not his father and mother shall die the death" (Exod. 20:12; 21:15); rather is it because He realizes that He is bound more to the mysteries of His

---

[3] Although there are many interpretations of the phrase "My hour is not yet come," that given by St. Cyril of Alexandria (c. 428) has become all but classical. After noting that Christ was not anxious to appear too soon as a wonder-worker, Cyril holds that Christ, out of deference to His Mother's request, anticipated the "hour" for working miracles: "In addition, Christ hereby shows that the deepest reverence is due to parents, since, out of reverence for His Mother, He grants that which He did not as yet wish to do. And the woman, who had such great influence in bringing about the miracle, prevailed by persuading the Lord [to do] what became Him as her Son" (*On the Gospel of John*, II, I; ed. Pusey, I, 202).

Father than to affection toward His Mother. But here there is no wrongful forsaking of parents. To the contrary, spiritual ties are taught to be more religious than such as are corporal. . . . And let no one suppose that there is here any offense against that filial piety which the Law prescribes. For if a man is to leave father and mother and to "cleave to his wife, and they are to be two in one flesh," then surely this mystery is justly realized in Christ and the Church (see Eph. 5:31). He could not therefore prefer parents to His own [Mystical] Body. Here, then, the Mother is not denied—as certain heretics would artfully make out—for she is acknowledged even from the Cross. Rather, preference over ties of flesh is given to a type of relationship which is prescribed from above. Again, there is nothing repugnant in this interpretation. For He is showing under the figure of His relations that the Church which believes is preferred to the Jews, of whom is Christ according to the flesh.

Exposition of Luke, 6, 36–38 (PL, 15, 1764; tr. with
some changes from Livius, p. 196 f.).

St. Jerome, 398

The Lord was engaged in the ministry of the word, in teaching the people, and in the office of preaching: His Mother and brethren come and stand outside and ask to speak to Him (see Mt. 12: 46-50). At this point someone tells our Savior that they are outside and asking for Him. Now, to my mind, the one who brought the message did not do so casually and with sincerity;

rather he was setting a trap for the Savior, to see whether He would prefer flesh and blood to His spiritual ministry. For this reason the Lord refuses to go out—not meaning to disown His Mother. But to answer the plotter, He stretches forth His hand towards His disciples, and says: "Behold my mother . . ." These are My Mother, who give birth to Me daily in the hearts of believers. These are My brethren, who do the works of My Father. By this, however, He did not—as Marcion and Manichaeus assert [4]—disown His Mother, so as to lend credence to the idea that He was born of a phantom; rather, He preferred His Apostles to His kindred that we too might prefer, where there is question of rival love, the spirit to the flesh.

Commentary on Matthew (PL, 26, 87).

---

[4] Marcion was a Gnostic of the Docetist variety (see p. 6). Manichaeus (Manes), a third century heretic from Persia, taught a basic dualism. Man's spirit is from God, the principle of light; his body from Satan, the principle of darkness. Hence, to beget children is to imprison the spirit in flesh, to circumscribe light by darkness. Manichaeism spread through the West and claimed for a time the great St. Augustine, who later became its most vigorous opponent. It was condemned by Leo the Great in a letter to the bishop of Astorga in Spain, where Manichaeism of the Priscillian variety was strong, and conciliar action was finally taken at the Council of Braga (561), a city which is now in modern Portugal (see DB, p. 111 and note 3). The spirit of Manes was revived by the Albigensians during the Middle Ages, was vigorously suppressed by the Inquisition as a menace to society, and in a milder form lives on in those religions which glorify the spirit of man at the expense of his material component. Against all these movements the words of the Christian Creed "who was born of the Virgin Mary" are as relevant today as they were against the Docetists in the early second century.

St. Augustine, 401

. . . More blessed, then, was Mary in receiving the faith of Christ, than in conceiving the flesh of Christ. For to her who said, "Blessed is the womb that bore thee and the paps that gave thee suck," He Himself made answer, "Yea, rather, blessed are they who hear the word of God and keep it" (Lk. 11:27-28). What in fact did their relationship profit His brethren, that is, His kinsmen according to the flesh, who believed not in Him? So too, even the close relationship of mother would have profited Mary nothing, had she not also more blessedly borne Christ in her heart than in her flesh. . . .

There is then no reason why virgins of God should be sad, because they too cannot, preserving their virginity, be mothers of flesh. For virginity could befittingly bring forth Him only who could have no father in His birth. Nevertheless that childbirth of one holy Virgin is the glory of all holy virgins. And they too are with Mary mothers of Christ, if they do His Father's will. For in this even Mary is with greater praise and blessedness Christ's Mother, according to the above-mentioned sentence: "Whoso doth the will of my Father who is in heaven, the same is my brother, and sister, and mother" (Mt. 12:50). All these relationships to Himself He sets forth spiritually in the people whom He has redeemed. He has as brethren and sisters, holy men and holy women, since these are co-heirs with Him in the heavenly inheritance. The whole Church is His mother, because she it is who brings forth His members, that is, His faithful by the grace of God. His mother too is every pious soul that does His Father's will by means of charity, which is most fruitful in those to whom it gives birth, until Christ be formed in them (see Gal. 4:15). Hence, Mary, in doing the will of God, is corporally only Christ's Mother, but spiritually both sister and mother.

On Holy Virginity, 3, 5 (PL, 40, 397 ff.;
tr. by Livius, p. 198 f.).

PART IV

DEVOTION TO MARY IN THE EAST

★

[Nestorius had denied that Mary was Theotokos, and the whole of the East arose to atone for this indignity to the Mother of God. Sermons in her honor resounded in the churches, feasts in her honor filled the liturgical calendar, and the flowering of Mary's cult was inevitable. St. Epiphanius had already warned against treating the Mother of God as a goddess and his warning would continue to restrain the faithful from giving to the Mother of God the adoration that belongs to God alone: ". . . God came down from heaven, the Word clothed Himself with flesh from a holy Virgin, not, assuredly, that the Virgin should be adored, nor to make her god, nor that we should offer sacrifice to her name, nor that, now after so many generations, women should once again be appointed priests. . . . He gave her no charge to minister baptism, to bless disciples, nor did He bid her to rule over the earth. But this only He willed, that she should be a work of sanctification, and should merit to be worthy of His kingdom. . . . Let Mary be had in honor, but let the Father, the Son and the Holy Spirit be adored. Let no one adore Mary" (*Heresies*, 79, 7 [GCS, 37, 482]). But this warning was not meant to restrain the faithful, under the guidance of their bishops, from celebrating with increasing solemnity the glories of Mary and from having recourse to her as Mother of God and Mother of men.]

1. SERMONS DELIVERED AGAINST NESTORIUS

[In the basilica of the Mother of God (the Theotokos), St. Cyril of Alexandria preached before the
Fathers of the Council of Ephesus what some regard as
the greatest Marian sermon in the whole of antiquity.
Some five months later (Jan. 6, 432), Theodotus of
Ancyra delivered at Ephesus his second homily on our
Lord's Nativity, which, along with his first homily, had
supposedly been read before the Council (but see ACO,
1, 1, 4, XXV). Even more famous is the sixth homily on
the same topic, although it is questionable whether it was
ever preached at Ephesus. Finally, we include the striking
"Loom of the Incarnation" motif of St. Proclus, soon to
succeed Nestorius in the Patriarchal See of Constantinople. This last was probably delivered in Constantinople
before Nestorius in the year 429.]

a. Mary as Mediatrix. St. Cyril of Alexandria. 431

Hail, then, from us, O holy mystical Trinity, who
has gathered us all together in this church of Mary,
the Mother of God. Hail, from us, Mary, Mother of
God, majestic treasure of the whole world, the lamp
unquenchable, the crown of virginity, the sceptre of
orthodoxy, the indestructible temple, the dwelling of
the Illimitable, Mother and Virgin, through whom
He is called in the holy Gospels "Blessed who cometh
in the name of the Lord." Hail, thou who didst contain Him in thy holy virginal womb, who cannot be
contained, thou through whom the Holy Trinity is
glorified and adored throughout the world; through
whom heaven rejoices, through whom angels and arch-

angels are glad; through whom devils are put to flight, through whom the tempter-devil fell from heaven; through whom the fallen creature is taken up into heaven; through whom all creation, held fast by the madness of idolatry, has come to the knowledge of the truth; through whom holy baptism has come to believers, and the oil of gladness; through whom churches are erected throughout the world; through whom the nations are brought to repentance. And what more shall I say? Through whom the only-begotten Son of God has shone forth, a light "to those who sat in darkness and in the shadow of death" (see Lk. 1:97); through whom the Prophets foretold, through whom the Apostles preached salvation to the nations; through whom the dead are raised, and kings reign.

Homily 4 (ACO, 1, 1, 2, 102–103).

b. *Mary, God's Eden. Theodotus of Ancyra, 432*

Radiant and paradoxical is the subject matter of the present festival [Christmas]: radiant, because it has brought salvation to all men; paradoxical, because it ran counter to nature's law. For nature no longer acknowledges a virgin after childbirth, but grace made her parent and kept her virgin; grace made her a mother and did not violate her virginity. . . . O earth unsown that flowered forth fruit that saves! O Virgin who surpasses Eden's garden of delights! . . . The Virgin is made more glorious than paradise. For paradise was cultivated by God; but Mary cultivated God Himself according to the flesh, willing as He did to be united to man's nature.

On the Nativity of Our Savior, 2 (ACO, 1, 1, 2, 80–81).

c. Mary Immaculate. Theodotus of Ancyra, c. 432

[The Greek text of this celebrated passage, which is not in Migne, has been seen in a tenth century manuscript by M. Jugie and is reproduced in part in his article "Immaculée Conception" (DTC, 7, 906 ff.). Our own translation is based on Jugie's French translation and on such key phrases as he supplies from the Greek.]

In place of the virgin Eve, mediatrix of death, a virgin has been filled with God's grace to be the minister of life; a virgin has been fashioned possessing the nature of a woman, but without part in her fault (malice); a virgin, innocent, without blemish, all-immaculate, inviolate, spotless, holy in soul and body, who has blossomed as a lily from among thorns, unlearned in the evil ways of Eve. . . . When yet unborn she was consecrated to God, and when born was offered to God as a sign of gratitude. . . . Clothed with divine grace as with a garment, her soul filled with a wisdom divine, in heart wedded to God, she received God in her womb, [she who is] in fact the Mother of God. . . .

Homily 6, On Holy Mary, Mother of God, and on the Holy Nativity of Christ, 11 (PG, 77, 1427).

d. *The Loom of the Incarnation. St. Proclus of Constantinople, c. 429*

The holy Mary has called us together, that undefiled treasure of virginity, the rational paradise of the second Adam, the workshop of the union of the natures, the market place for the salutary exchange, the bridal chamber wherein the Word espoused flesh . . . the most pure fleece of heavenly rain (Judges 6:37), from which the Shepherd clothed the sheep—handmaid and Mother, Virgin and heaven, the only bridge of God to men.

She is the awe-inspiring loom of the Incarnation, whereon in a way unspeakable was woven the garment of the hypostatic union, with the Holy Spirit as weaver; the overshadowing power from above, the connecting thread (*erithos*); the ancient fleece of Adam, the wool; the undefiled flesh from the Virgin, the threaded woof; the shuttle, the immeasurable grace of her who bore, with the Logos as Artist. . . .

> *Encomium on the All-Holy Mary, Mother of God*, 1, 1
> (ACO, 1, 1, I, 103).

2. THE INVOCATION OF THE MOTHER OF GOD

[Just when Christians began to invoke Mary directly is difficult to say. From the earliest times her secondary role in man's redemption was acknowledged in the recurrent theme of Mary as the second Eve. And it was as Mediatrix with Christ, who is alone Mediator, that her praises were sung from the time of St. Justin Martyr. Such being the fact, it was inevitable that Christians should turn to Mary and pray that she continue her role as Mediatrix in their

E

regard. In this sense the invocation "Holy Mary, Mother of God, pray for us sinners now and at the hour of our death" came to be the obvious complement to the Angel's salutation: "Hail Mary, full of grace. The Lord is with thee; blessed art thou amongst women, and blessed is the fruit of thy womb." Tradition has it that the complement was first added by the Church of Alexandria, at the time of the Nestorian denial of the Theotokos. In an Ethiopic hymn sung in the Church of Axum, a daughter Church of Alexandria, the following verses follow closely upon each other: "*Blessed art thou of women, and blessed is the fruit of thy womb.* . . . All the saints shall say to thee as is their due, *Pray for us, O thou who art full of grace*" (see *Dublin Review*, 10 [1868], 325 ff., in which this hymn is reproduced in full and assigned to a period between the Councils of Ephesus in 431 and Chalcedon in 451).]

a. The Akathistos Hymn of the Byzantine Liturgy

[From the opening stanza it would appear that this hymn was written to commemorate the deliverance of the city of Constantinople from the barbarians in the year 626. It has been suggested, however, that this stanza was merely added to the already existing hymn on the above-mentioned occasion, and that the hymn itself is from the pen of the early sixth century Greek hymnographer, Romanus the Singer. The hymn is made up of twenty-four stanzas of alternating lengths and was sung standing, whence the name *Akathistos* (*Not-Sitting*) *Hymn*. Accepting the opening stanza as introductory, we cite the first, the twenty-third and the twenty-fourth stanzas for the testimony they offer to the belief of Christians in the intercessory powers of the Mother of God.]

To thee, unconquered Queen, I thy city from danger freed an offering of thanks inscribe. O Forthbringer of God! Yet for thy unconquerable might free me from all hurt that I may sing to thee:

HAIL! BRIDE UNBRIDED

I. An angel chieftain was sent from Heaven to greet the Forth-bringer of God with Hail! Then seeing thee, O Lord, take flesh he is wonder-rapt, and standing crieth out with no lips of flesh to her:

Hail! by whom true hap had dawned.

Hail! by whom mishap has waned.

Hail! sinful Adam's recalling.

Hail! Eve's tears redeeming.

Hail! height untrodden by thought of men.

Hail! depth unscanned by angel's ken.

Hail! for the kingly throne thou art.

Hail! for who beareth all thou bearest?

Hail! O star that bore the Sun.

Hail! the womb of God enfleshed.

Hail! through whom things made are all new made.

Hail! through whom becomes a Babe their Maker.

Hail! through whom the Maker is adored.

HAIL! BRIDE UNBRIDED

XII. All we who psalm thy Son give praise to thee as to the living temple, O God's Forth-bringer; when within thy womb dwelt the Lord who holdeth all in his hand, he hallowed, honoured thee, and taught all to cry to thee:

Hail! tabernacle of God and the Word.

Hail! holy beyond all holy ones.

Hail! ark gilded by the Holy Ghost.

Hail! unfailing treasure-house of life.

Hail! precious diadem of godly Sovereigns.

Hail! worshipful honour of a worthy priesthood.

Hail! the Church's unassailable tower.

Hail! indestructible wall of the Kingdom.

Hail! thou whereby war-trophies are set up.

Hail! whereby foes are stricken.

Hail! my body's healing.

Hail! my soul's saving.

HAIL! BRIDE UNBRIDED

O Mother whom all must hymn, O thou who hast brought forth the Word most holy beyond all the holiest, take our present offering, keep all from every hurt, and deliver from all wrath to come those who cry to thee:

ALLELUIA.

Tr. Rev. Vincent McNabb, O. P., *The Akathistos Hymn* [Blackfriars, Oxford, 1947].

b. St. Germanus of Constantinople, c. 717

[In the year 717 the siege of the city of Constantinople by Leo the Isaurian was lifted through the intercession of the Blessed Mother of God. St. Germanus, the Patriarch, ordered a feast to be celebrated in Mary's honor, in which the Akathistos hymn was sung. In the following sermon, his own invocation of our Lady rivals that of the Akathistos itself.]

O Lady, all-chaste, all-good, rich in mercy, comfort of Christians, tender consoler of the afflicted, the ever-open refuge of sinners, do not leave us destitute of thy assistance. . . . Shelter us under the wings of thy goodness. By thy intercession watch over us. O unfailing hope of Christians, hold forth to us eternal life. . . . For no one, Lady all-holy, is saved except through thee, all-holy one. . . . No one, Lady most chaste, is favored with any gift except through thee. No one, Lady most venerable, is given the merciful gift of grace except through thee. . . . After thy Son, who more than thee has the interests of mankind at heart? Who more than thee protects and sustains us in our bitter sorrow? . . . Who like to thee excels as suppliant for sinners? . . . At the very invocation of thy holy name, thou dost turn aside from thy servants the attacks of that most evil enemy, and keep them safe and unharmed.

Sermon 9, At the Consecration of a Church to the Holy Mother of God (PG, 98, 377–381).

3. THE FEAST OF MARY'S FALLING ASLEEP

[There is no certain evidence of a liturgical feast in honor of Mary prior to the fifth century. This will not appear strange if it is remembered that the feast of Christmas itself can be dated back only to the fourth century. In a sermon preached by St. Proclus at the time of the Council of Ephesus (431), reference is made to "the Virgin's festival" [PG, 65, 679], which may well have commemorated in a global way the various privileges of Mary, a primitive "Mary-Day." The Greek historian

Nicephorus relates that the Emperor Maurice (c. 600) ordered that the "Falling Asleep" of the Virgin should be celebrated on the fifteenth of August (*Ecclesiastical History*, 15, 4, 14 [PG, 147, 44]). This, however, may merely indicate a change in the date of its celebration. Of more importance is the significance of this feast, which in Rome was called "the feast of Mary's Dormition" (c. 700) and which was celebrated in Gaul (c. 800) under the title of "the Assumption." The object of the feast as celebrated in the East will appear from the following extracts, while the problems which the feast raised in the West will be considered in Part V.]

a. St. Germanus of Constantinople, c. 720

In accord with what has been written, "thou art beautiful" (Cant. 2:13), and thy virginal body is wholly saintly, wholly chaste, wholly the dwelling place of God; with the result that thereafter it is wholly free from dissolution into dust, changeless in all that is human, it is exalted to immortal life, that very same body, now living and glorified, and sharing without loss in the perfection of life; inasmuch as it was impossible that the vessel which had received God, the living temple of the sacred deity of the Only-begotten, should be held fast by death's sepulchre. Therefore, O Mother of God, we believe that thou goest about among us.

On the Falling Asleep of the Mother of God, 1 (PG, 98, 345).

b. St. Andrew of Crete, d. 740

She who has introduced into heaven that which is dust, strips off the dust and lays aside the veil she has carried from her birth, and restores to the earth what is kin to earth. She who gave life to Life migrates up to a new life, to a place where life originates and life is indestructible. . . . And, last of all phenomena, that which appears to our eyes rises up and in a spiritual way goes along with that which is spiritual in the manner known to Him who of old linked the two together, and after dissolving them united them anew. . . . See if a more astounding miracle can be discovered than the marvel that was accomplished so incredibly in her. . . . A spectacle truly new it was, and beyond human thinking; the woman who surpassed the heavens in her purity, crossed the threshold of heaven's sanctuary; the Virgin who surpassed the Seraphim by the marvel of her divine maternity, drew close to the primal nature, God the Creator of all things; the Mother who had given birth to Life itself, crowned her life by an end in harmony with her maternity. . . . For as the womb of the Mother knew not corruption, so too the flesh of the dead did not perish. . . .

> *On the Falling Asleep of the Most Holy Mother of God*, 1 (PG, 97, 1080–81).

c. St. John Damascene, d. 749

[St. John of Damascus in Syria is the last of the Greek Fathers. Like St. Ephrem the Syrian, he is one of the outstanding liturgical poets of the East. On the occasion of the definition of the Immaculate Conception and, more recently, of the Assumption of our Lady, no great protest was heard from the Churches of the East. The reason is to be found in the eloquent testimony to both dogmas given by John Damascene, acknowledged today in the great Churches of the East as the champion of Orthodoxy. In every attempt to bring about union between Rome and the East, the teaching of Damascene has served as a point of agreement; and should reunion eventually come, St. John Damascene and the Lady of whom he sings will play an important part, subordinate only to that of Christ, the Mediator par excellence.]

. . . There was need that this dwelling meet for God, this undug well of remission's waters, this unploughed field of heaven's bread, this unwatered vineyard of immortality's wine, this olive tree of the Father's compassion, ever green and fair and fruitful, be not imprisoned in the hollows of the earth. Rather, just as the holy and incorrupt body that had been born of her, the body that was united hypostatically to God the Word, rose from the tomb on the third day, so she too should be snatched from the grave and the Mother restored to her Son; and, as He had descended to her, so she should be carried up . . . to heaven. There was need that she, who had entertained God the Word in the guest chamber of her womb, should be brought home to the dwelling of her Son; and just as the Lord said that He must be in the place that belongs to His Father, so the Mother had to take up her abode in the palace of her Son, in the house of the Lord, in the court of the house of our God. There was need that the body of her, who in childbirth had preserved her virginity without stain, be preserved incorrupt even after death. There was need that she, who had carried her Creator as a babe on her bosom, should linger lovingly in the dwelling of her God. There was need that the bride, whom the Father had betrothed to Himself, should live in the bridal chamber of heaven. There was need that she, who had looked so closely on her very own Son on the Cross, who there felt in her heart the sword-pangs of sorrow which in bearing Him she had been spared, should look upon Him seated with His Father. There was need that the Mother of God should enter into the possessions of her Son and, as Mother of God and handmaid, be reverenced by all creation. . . . For the Son has enslaved all creation to His Mother.

> *On the Falling Asleep of the Mother of God,*
> 2, 14 (PG, 96, 740–41).

4. The Feast of Mary's Conception

[It is quite possible that this feast, under the title "the Conception of [by] St. Ann," originally commemorated the physical miracle of a woman, beyond the age of child-bearing, conceiving a daughter, just as St. Elizabeth had conceived John the Baptist. A transfer in emphasis from the physical miracle wrought in Ann to the miracle of grace wrought by God in the soul of Mary, was inevitable in the light of the eulogies to Mary already seen. Mary is the "incorruptible timber" out of which was hewn the tabernacle of Christ's sinless body (St. Hippolytus, p. 15); she is "God's Eden, in whom there is no tree of knowledge, and no serpent that harms" (St. Ephrem, p. 22). Her perfect beauty and spotlessness find their exemplar in Christ, her purity in that of the Father (St. Ephrem, p. 22). At the time of the Council of Ephesus, she is hailed as "innocent, without blemish, immaculate, inviolate, spotless, holy in soul and body, who has blossomed as a lily from among thorns, unlearned in the evil ways of Eve" (p. 52). A later version of the Akathistos Hymn states quite briefly what will be the central object of the feast of Mary's Conception in the years to come: "The author of heaven and earth, having formed thee without stain, was pleased to inhabit thee" (see *The Sacramentary*, I. Shuster, 5 [London, 1930], 338). It is this aspect of the Conception by Ann that is underscored in the passages that follow. Although taken from sermons that commemorate the birth of Mary, the first two excerpts deal more particularly with Mary's Conception or first fashioning in the womb of Ann.]

a. St. Andrew of Crete, d. 740

Today the created temple of the Creator of all things is built. . . . Today . . . Adam, in offering the first fruits to the Lord for us and from us, selects as first fruits Mary, who, out of the whole mass that had spoiled, remained unspoiled; from whom the bread was made for the redemption of the race. . . . Today, mankind is pure and nobly born and receives the gift of its original divine creation, and returns to its [former] self. And that beauty and loveliness which was darkened by man's birth in obscurity and in evil, that same beauty and loveliness nature brings to the Mother of the Beautiful One at her birth and receives a formation that is supreme and a loveliness that is divine. [In Mary] nature's formation becomes in reality a restoration—and the restoration, a deification—which in turn is a replica of the original deification. In a word, today there is begun the refashioning of our nature, and the world that has grown old, by undergoing a transformation that is in form divine, receives the beginnings of a second creation that is of God.

On the Nativity of the Mother of God, 1 (PG, 97, 809–812).

b. St. John Damascene, d. 749

O most sacred daughter of Joachim and Ann, who wast hidden from principalities and powers as well as from the fiery darts of the wicked one, who didst dwell in the bridal chamber of the Holy Spirit and wast kept without stain, in order to become the bride of God and God's Mother by nature. . . .

On the Nativity of the Mother of God (PG, 96, 672).

Today Eden receives the rational paradise of the new Adam, in which the condemnation is lifted, and in which the Tree of Life is planted. . . . In this paradise there was no serpent. . . . For the only-begotten Son of God, being God, of the same substance as God, from this virgin and pure earth formed himself into a man.

On the Falling Asleep of the Mother of God, 2 (PG, 96 725).

PART V

CONTROVERSY IN THE WEST

★

1. The Assumption of the Mother of God

[As early as the close of the fourth century, St. Epiphanius was called upon to defend the Mother of God against the blasphemous and heretical suggestion that Mary lived with St. John as wife rather than mother. By way of an *argumentum ad hominem*, St. Epiphanius declares that Scripture tells us nothing of Mary's history subsequent to Pentecost: "But if any think that I am in error, let them search the Scriptures and they will find there no mention of her death, whether she died or whether she did not die, or whether she was buried or whether she was not buried. . . . For my own part, I do not dare to speak, but I keep my own thoughts, and I observe silence. . . . For Scripture has outstripped the human mind and left the matter uncertain for the sake of that precious vessel without compare, to prevent anyone from harboring carnal thoughts in her regard. . . ." (*Heresies*, 78, 11 [GCS, 37, 462]). Actually, the Catholic dogma of the Assumption does not rest on any scriptural account of her death, nor, for that matter, on any traditional account of her actual translation from earth to heaven. Rather, as one Anglican writer says of an apocryphal account of the Assumption: "The belief was never founded on that story. The story was founded on the belief. The belief which was universal, required a defined shape, and that shape at length it found" (J. B. Mozley, *Reminiscences of Oriol College and the Oxford*

64

Movement, II, 368). It is the failure to grasp this truth which appears to explain in part the hesitancy of the author of the Pseudo-Jerome, who, quite probably, is Paschasius Radbertus (died c. 865).]

a. The Reluctance of the Pseudo-Jerome, c. 865

With regard to the Assumption of the same Blessed Mother of God and ever Virgin Mary, your lady-ship has asked how it came about. . . . [From the apocrypha] nothing can be learned with certainty other than the fact that on this day she gloriously left the body. . . . Some of ours doubt whether she was assumed along with the body, or whether on her de-parture she quitted the body. After all, it is not known how or when or by what persons her most holy body was removed from that place, or where it was taken or whether she arose; although some would like to assert that she is already risen and is, in heaven, clothed together with Christ in the blessed [garment] of im-mortality. . . . Better, however, that we leave the whole matter to God, for whom nothing is impossible, than that we should be willing to define rashly on our own authority something which we may not prove. . . . Since nothing is impossible to God, neither do we deny that this [the bodily Assumption] did take place in the case of blessed Mary, although for reasons of caution (for faith's sake) it would be more fitting to hold it with filial longing than to define unadvisedly what is known only with difficulty.

Letter 9, To Paula and Eustochium on the Assumption
(PL, 30, 123–24).

b. The Affirmation of the Pseudo-Augustine, c. 778

[The author of the following treatise on the Assumption may possibly be Autpertus of Ratramnus (d. 778). This treatise prescinds entirely from all apocryphal accounts of Mary's death, burial and resurrection, and appeals to a more developed Christian sense which tends to associate Mary's destiny with that of her Son. We have seen the classical expression of this tendency in St. John Damascene, and we shall see it again in the famous dictum ascribed to Scotus in his defense of the Immaculate Conception: "God could, it was fitting that He should, therefore He did—*Potuit, decuit, ergo fecit*" (see below p. 72). This principle of fitness or suitability finds no better expression than in the present treatise of Pseudo-Augustine.]

2. What, then, is to be said about the death of Mary, what of her Assumption, except that we must search with our understanding for reasons that are compatible with the truth, and then the truth will be its own witness, apart from which even proof must be without value. Now, mindful of man's lot, we are not afraid to admit that she underwent death for a time, a death which her Son as well, both God and Man, in accord with the lot of men, certainly endured. . . .

4. Therefore, Mary, though she shares in Eve's hardships, does not share in the pangs of childbirth. For her singular holiness and her singular grace, by which in a unique fashion she was deemed worthy to bear God, merited this [favor]. . . . The totality of the world shows forth the extent of Christ's power;

Mary's integrity shows forth the extent of her grace. What so strange, then, if, in this great variety [of privileges], we say that she suffered death, the common lot of men, and yet that she was not bound down by death's chains, she through whom God willed to be born and to share the substance of flesh? Surely this will not be impious. For we know that Jesus can do all things. . . .

6. The throne of God, the bridal chamber of the Lord of heaven, the dwelling and tabernacle of Christ is worthy to be there where He Himself is. . . . That the most sacred body, then, from which Christ assumed flesh . . . was handed over to be the food of worms, I cannot bring myself to believe; that is why I shudder to speak of that corruption which is man's common lot, and of worms [commingling] with the resulting dust.

8. When all these considerations are weighed, I hold that we must confess with good reason that Mary is in Christ and with Christ: in Christ, because in Him we live and move and have our being; with Christ gloriously assumed to the joys of eternity. . . .

9. If anyone shall choose to gainsay the Assumption, since he would not deny that Christ could bring it about, let him advance reasons to show that it would not become Christ to will to do it, and therefore that it was not done. . . . And if he shall show that he truly knows the mind of God in the matter, I will begin to accept from him what otherwise I have not dared to imagine. . . . If, then, what I have written

is true, to Thee, O Christ, I give thanks that I could not bring myself to imagine anything of Thy holy Virgin Mother than what seems filial and proper. If, then, I have spoken as I should, do Thou, O Christ, Thou and Thine, approve, I beseech; but if amiss, do Thou and Thine forgive me.

On the Assumption of the Blessed Virgin Mary
(PL, 40, 1140–48).

2. THE IMMACULATE CONCEPTION

[In the middle of the twelfth century, the feast of our Lady's Conception was introduced into Lyons in France. Five centuries earlier, the same feast under the title of "the Conception of St. Ann" was already popular in the Church of the East. Nor did the feast ever meet with any opposition on the part of the faithful in France or, later, in the whole of Europe. It is an irony of history that the first to challenge directly the doctrinal import of the feast of our Lady's Conception is St. Bernard, whose lyricism in writing of the Mother of God has merited him the title, "Mary's Troubadour."]

a. St. Bernard of Clairvaux, 1153

[In a letter to the canons of Lyons, St. Bernard censures them for introducing the feast of our Lady's Conception. And yet, Bernard himself insists that the "woman" of the Proto-Gospel (Gen. 3:15), who was to be at enmity with the serpent and who was to gain a resounding victory over him, was in fact Mary. "To whom" asks Bernard, "was this victory reserved if not to Mary?" (*On the Words "Missus est*," Homily 2, 4 [PL, 183, 63]). The implications of the Proto-Gospel will be spelled out in the bull that defines the dogma of the Immaculate Conception (see p. 82). They are lost on St. Bernard, however, for reasons that he himself gives. Still, one point should be stressed: St. Bernard is prepared to relinquish his view if the Church should ever decide otherwise.]

But the Mother of the Lord, you say, is to be highly honored. And you advise me well. However, the Queen's honor prefers discretion. . . . By all means honor the integrity of her flesh, the sanctity of her life. Marvel that a virgin should be fruitful, and reverence her divine offspring. Sing the praises of one who knew not concupiscence when she conceived or pain when she gave birth. . . . Sing a Magnificat to her who is the Inventrix of grace, the Mediatrix of salvation and the Reparatrix of the world; in a word, exalt her who is exalted above the choirs of angels in the kingdom of heaven. These are the songs that the Church sings to me in her honor, and these same songs she has taught me to sing to others. . . .

Unquestionably, the Mother of the Lord was holy before she was born; nor is the holy Church in any way mistaken when she regards as holy the very day of her birth. . . . I think, too, that an even more abundant blessing of grace was shed upon her not only to sanctify her in birth but also to keep her through life free of any sin. . . .

What further honor are we to suppose as warranted? The honor due her Conception, they say, which preceded her honorable birth. . . . But how can there be holiness in conception? Does one mean

F

that she was holy before she was conceived, in the sense that she was conceived holy . . . just as she is said to have been sanctified in the womb with the result that her birth was holy? But she could not have been holy before she existed since she did not exist before she was conceived. Or did sanctity perhaps commingle with conception at the time of the marital embrace, so that she was sanctified and conceived at one and the same time? But this is surely unreasonable. For how can there be any sanctity without the Holy Spirit, or do you mean that the Holy Spirit was a partner to the sin [of concupiscence]? Or are we to assume that there was no sin where lust was not absent? [5] Or will someone perhaps say that Mary was conceived, not of a man, but of the Holy Ghost? But this is something hitherto unheard of. . . . Therefore, the Lord Jesus alone was conceived of the Holy Spirit since He alone was holy both before and after conception. With His exception, the following humble and truthful confession of one man in his own regard has application to all who are born of Adam: "In iniquities was I conceived and in sins my mother brought me forth."

---

[5] Many theologians of this period were of the persuasion that concupiscence, the material element of original sin, was transmitted by way of intercourse, in which the evil of concupiscence, although not culpable, was never wholly absent. This explanation of the Church's dogma on the transmission of original sin by way of generation is in no sense part of the Church's dogma, and has long been rejected by Catholic theologians. In this rejection a deeper intelligence of the dogma of the Immaculate Conception has played no small part.

And yet what I have written has been said surely without prejudice to one of maturer wisdom. And this applies especially to the authority of the Roman Church. To her examination I reserve the whole matter just as I do other matters of this kind. If my understanding in any way differs from hers, I am prepared to correct my judgment.

Letter 174 (PL, 182, 333 ff.).

b. St. Thomas Aquinas, d. 1274

[St. Thomas never wrote a formal treatise on the Blessed Mother. His own views on the Immaculate Conception are rather incidental to his treatment of Christ's sinlessness. For this reason he was content to accept the conclusion of St. Bernard; of St. Albert the Great, his teacher; and of St. Bonaventure, his contemporary. He accepted as well a formulation of the question that unfortunately prejudiced the answer. The question was not whether Mary could have been preserved free from original sin at the moment her soul was infused into her body. Rather it was, "Whether the Blessed Virgin was sanctified before she was animated" (i.e., before her body was animated by the soul). And it is to this question that St. Thomas replies in the third part of the *Summa Theologica*.]

I reply by saying that the sanctification of the Blessed Virgin cannot be understood to have taken place before her animation, and this for two reasons: first, indeed, because the sanctification of which we are speaking is nothing else but the cleansing from original sin. . . . Now, the guilt of sin cannot be

washed away except by means of grace, whose subject is only a rational creature. And, therefore, before
the infusion of the rational soul the Blessed Virgin
was not sanctified. Secondly, since it is only a rational
soul that is susceptible of guilt, the foetus that is conceived before the infusion of the soul is not subject
to guilt. And so, no matter how the Blessed Virgin
might have been sanctified before animation, she
would never have contracted the stain of original
guilt, and would, therefore, never have needed that
redemption and salvation which is through Christ, of
which St. Matthew writes: "He shall save his people
from their sins" (Mt. 1:21). But it is not suitable that
Christ should not be "the Savior of all men," as it is
stated in I Tim. 4:10. Hence, it remains that the
sanctification of the Blessed Virgin took place after
her animation.

Summa Theol., III, q. 27, a. 2.

c. John Duns Scotus, d. 1308

[Almost two centuries earlier, Eadmer of Canterbury,
a disciple of St. Anselm, had argued to the fact of the
Immaculate Conception from God's ability to bring it
about. The famous formula *"Potuit, decuit, ergo fecit—*
God could, it was fitting that He should, therefore He
did,"* although attributed to Scotus, is actually a gloss on
the following words of Eadmer: *"Potuit plane. Si igitur
voluit, fecit—*He surely could have; if therefore He willed
it, He did it" (*Tract. de conc. S. Mariæ*, PL, 159, 305).
However, it remained for Scotus, a compatriot of Eadmer,
to show that Christ by preserving His Mother free from

original sin actually redeemed her by the most perfect act
of mediation.]

He who is the most perfect mediator must have a
most perfect act of mediation in regard to some person
on whose behalf he exercises his mediatorial office.
Now Christ is a most perfect mediator. Therefore
Christ exercised the most perfect degree of mediation
in favor of some creature or person in whose behalf
He was Mediator. But He had no more exalted relationship to any person than to the Blessed Virgin
Mary. Therefore. . . . But this could not be, had He
not merited for her preservation from original sin.

Quaestiones disputatae de Immac. Concep.
(ed. Ad Claras Aquas, 1904, p. 14).

To the question, I say that (1) God could have
brought it about that Mary should never have been
in original sin; (2) He could also have brought it
about that she should remain in sin only for a single
second; (3) He could also have brought it about that
she should remain in sin for some time and only at the
last moment that she should be cleansed. Now, which
of these three possible courses was actually adopted
is known to God. If there is no conflict with the
authority of Scripture or with the authority of the
Church, that course seems probable which renders
greater honor to Mary.

Ibid., p. 16.

d. The Attitude of the Holy See. Sixtus IV, 1471–1484

[As the controversy between the followers of St. Thomas and those of Scotus waxed stronger, devotion to our Lady's Immaculate Conception increased. Further impetus was given by the following constitution of Sixtus IV.]

When, with that deep insight that comes of devout contemplation, we search and discover the sublime proofs of those merits which cause the Queen of heaven, the glorious Virgin Mother of God, raised upon her heavenly throne, to outshine like the morning star all other constellations . . . we deem it fitting, and even our duty, to invite by means of indulgences and the remission of sins all the faithful of Christ to offer thanks and praise to God . . . for the wondrous Conception of this same Immaculate Virgin, and to celebrate or to be present at Masses and at other divine functions which have been instituted in the Church for this purpose. In this way, the faithful will, through the intercession and merits of the same Virgin, become more docile to divine grace.

Constitution *Cum Praeexcelsa*, 1476 (DB, 734).

[The irenic tone that characterized the controversy between the great Schoolmen gave way to bitter invective in not a few of their disciples. The charge of heresy is not to be made lightly, and Sixtus IV had to intervene a second time. Once again the attitude of the Holy See towards the Immaculate Conception is made clear, but no dogmatic definition is as yet made.]

Although the holy Roman Church publicly and solemnly celebrates the feast of the Conception of the inviolate and ever Virgin Mary, and has arranged a special and proper Office for the feast, we have learned that some preachers from different Orders, in their sermons to the people throughout various cities and districts, have up to the present unblushingly asserted in public and are daily continuing to preach that all sin mortally or are heretics who hold or assert that the same glorious and immaculate Mother of God was conceived without the stain of original sin; and that those sin mortally who celebrate the Office of this same Immaculate Conception or listen to the sermons of those who affirm that she was conceived without stain of this kind. . . . By the tenor of these presents, we reprove and condemn with apostolic authority assertions of this kind as false and erroneous and as wholly foreign to the truth. . . . [We reprehend as well those] who shall dare to assert that those who hold the contrary view—namely, that the glorious Virgin Mary was conceived with original sin—are guilty of the crime of heresy or of mortal sin, since the matter has not been decided as yet by the Roman Church and Apostolic See.

Constitution *Grave Nimis,* 1483 (DB, 737).

PART VI

FROM THE COUNCIL OF TRENT TO PIUS IX

1. THE COUNCIL OF TRENT, 1545–1563

[There are only two explicit references to the Virgin Mary in the numerous decrees and canons of the Council of Trent, and even these two are not directed against the Protestant reformers. Martin Luther refused to distinguish between true and exaggerated devotion to the Mother of God, and set the tone of future Protestant denials by branding all devotion to the saints and to Mary, their Queen, as idolatry. And yet Luther never completely rejected the Church's teaching on the prerogatives of the Blessed Virgin Mary.[6] This will explain why the Council of Trent confines itself to a doctrinal pronouncement of Mary's sinlessness which is actually directed against the older Pelagians (see p. 33), and in its decree on original

---

[6] As late as the year 1527, seven years after his excommunication, Luther expressed the following sentiments in a sermon to commemorate the feast of the Immaculate Conception: "We could not say to her: 'Blessed art thou,' if she had at any time been subject to malediction. Again it is only right and proper that the person from whom Christ was to take flesh which would vanquish all sin should herself be preserved free from sin. For 'blessed' in its proper sense means that which is gifted with divine grace, namely, that which is without sin" ("*Kirchenpostille,*" in Luther's *Sammtliche Werke,* Erlangen ed. 1828, 15, 55). The editor of this edition notes on p. 54 that after 1527 this section of Luther's sermon was expunged from later editions until restored by himself.

sin merely makes it clear that it has no intention of including the Blessed Virgin.]

a. Mary's Sinlessness

Canon 23. If anyone shall say that a man once justified . . . can through the whole of life avoid all sins,
even though they be venial, except by a special privilege of God, as the Church holds to have been the
case with the Blessed Virgin, let him be anathema.

Session VI, 1547 (DB, 833).

b. Her Exemption from the Decree on Original Sin

This same holy Synod declares that it is not its intention to include in this decree, where there is question of original sin, the blessed and immaculate Virgin
Mary, Mother of God. Rather, the constitutions of
Sixtus of happy memory are to be followed. . . .

Session V, 1546 (DB, 792).

2. PAUL IV: MARY'S PERPETUAL VIRGINITY, 1555

[This document is directed against the Socinians or
Unitarians, who denied the distinction of Persons in the
Trinity, the fact of the Incarnation and the virginity of
the Blessed Mother.]

In a spirit of paternal severity we are anxious to
admonish each and everyone who has heretofore asserted, taught or believed . . . that the same most
Blessed Virgin Mary is not truly the Mother of God
or that she did not always retain the integrity of her

virginity, that is, before birth, during birth, and continuously after birth. . . .

Constitution Cum quorundam (DB, 993).

3. PIUS V: THE ERRORS OF BAIUS, 1567

Error 73. No one, with the exception of Christ, is without original sin. Therefore, the Blessed Virgin died because of the sin contracted from Adam, and all her afflictions in this life, no less than those of the rest of the just, were the punishment of actual or original sin.

DB, 1073.

4. ALEXANDER VII: THE IMMACULATE CONCEPTION, 1661

Ancient is the piety of the Christian faithful toward our Blessed Mother, the Virgin Mary. They believe that her soul, in the first moment of creation and infusion into the body, was, by a special grace and privilege of God, and in consideration of the merits of Jesus Christ her Son, the Redeemer of the human race, preserved free from the stain of original sin. And it is in this sense that the faithful cherish and celebrate with solemn rites the feast of her Conception. . . .

Bull Solicitudo omnium, 8 Dec., 1661 (DB, 1100).

5. ALEXANDER VIII: THE CONDEMNATION OF JANSENISM, 1690

Error 24. The offering which the Blessed Virgin Mary made in the temple on the day of her purification with two young turtledoves, one as a holocaust, the other as a sin offering, is sufficient evidence that she needed purification, and that her Son, who was presented, was also marked with the stain of His Mother, according to the words of the Law.

Decree of Holy Office, 7 Dec., 1690 (DB, 1314).

6. THE SIXTH PROVINCIAL COUNCIL OF BALTIMORE: MARY IMMACULATE AS PATRONESS OF THE UNITED STATES, 1846

[In 1792, Archbishop Carroll dedicated the primatial see of Baltimore to our Lady of the Assumption. On May 13, 1846, in the Cathedral of the Assumption, twenty-three bishops from twenty dioceses of the United States unanimously sponsored a decree which proposed the Mother of God, under the title of the Immaculate Conception, as Patroness of the United States (cf. *Concilia Provincialia Baltimori*, 1829–49 [Baltimore, 1857], 244). Confirmation was given by Pius IX on February 7, 1847, less than eight years before he solemnly defined the dogma. At the close of the Seventh Provincial Council of Baltimore, the following salutation was added to the *Te Deum:* "Eternal honor to the most Blessed Virgin Mary, conceived without original sin, Patroness of these Provinces!" The following excerpt is taken from the pastoral letter drawn up in the Sixth Provincial Council.]

We take this occasion, brethren, to communicate to you the determination, unanimously adopted by us, to place ourselves and all entrusted to our care throughout the United States, under the special patronage of the Mother of God, whose Immaculate Conception is venerated by the piety of the faithful throughout the

Catholic Church. . . . To her then we commend you, in confidence that through the one Mediator of God and men, the man Christ Jesus, Who gave Himself a redemption for all, she will obtain for us grace and salvation. The grace of our Lord Jesus Christ be with you all. Amen!

The Catholic Almanac for 1847 (Baltimore, 1847), p. 33.

PART VII

THE DOGMA OF THE IMMACULATE CONCEPTION

★

Pius IX: Bull *Ineffabilis Deus*, Dec. 8, 1854

[Before the definition of the dogma itself, Piux IX dwells at some length on the reasons that convinced him that the doctrine of the Immaculate Conception could be defined as a truth revealed by God. The attitude of the Holy See over the space of some four hundred years showed the official mind of the Roman Church, "which is the Mother of all Churches." That attitude was always one of encouragement and even of initiative in inviting the faithful to celebrate the feast of Mary's Conception with becoming splendor. At the Council of Trent, the Church in ecumenical assembly had made it clear that her teaching on the universality of original sin was not meant to include the Blessed Virgin Mary. Finally, the universal belief of the faithful, together with the assurance of the bishops of the Catholic world that the truth was divinely revealed, removed all possibility of doubt. For the bishops, in union with the Holy See, are the divinely constituted teachers of the Church, while the words of Christ, "He that heareth you, heareth me," guarantee the belief of the faithful. Strictly speaking, this consent of the bishops was enough to warrant the dogma. Piux IX, however, was conscious that his action would be open to the scrutiny of the non-Catholic world. Some would demand that the dogma be established from Sacred Scripture, others that it be proven historically. Out of consideration for such, perhaps, the Pope appeals to Scripture, not as it is contained in the pages of a written though inspired book, but as the relevant passages of Scripture have been understood and preached by the Church herself through the voice of its Fathers and great ecclesiastical writers, who are the witnesses of the faith in their age. It is this section of the bull that we now cite.]

1. THE ARGUMENT FROM TRADITION

The Fathers and writers of the Church, well versed in the heavenly Scriptures, had nothing more at heart in the books which they put together in order to explain the Scriptures, vindicate the dogmas and instruct the faithful, than to emulate one another in declaring and proclaiming in a remarkable variety of ways the Virgin's exalted sanctity, her dignity and freedom from all stain of sin, and her celebrated victory over the most hateful enemy of the human race.

a. Genesis 3:15

When, therefore, they cited the words: "I will place enmity between thee and the woman, between thy seed and her seed"—words in which, at the beginning of the world, God announced His merciful remedies, prepared for the regeneration of mankind, checked the brazenness of the lying serpent, and marvelously raised up the hope of our race—they taught that in this divine prophecy the merciful Redeemer of the human race, the only-begotten Son of God, Christ Jesus, was clearly foretold, and that his most Blessed

Mother, the Virgin Mary, was designated, and that the enmity of both against the serpent was at the same time remarkably expressed. Therefore as Christ, the Mediator of God and men, in the human nature which He assumed, blotted out the handwriting of the decree which stood against us, and fastened it triumphantly to the Cross, so the most holy Virgin, bound to Him by a most intimate and indissoluble bond, with Him and through Him displayed eternal enmity towards the malignant serpent, and, gaining a resounding victory over him, crushed his head with her immaculate foot. . . .

b. Mary, the Second Eve

Therefore, to vindicate the original innocence and justice of the Mother of God, they [the Fathers] not only compare her to Eve while still a virgin, still innocent, still inviolate and still undeceived by the deadly snares of the treacherous serpent, but they have also preferred her to Eve with a wonderful variety of expressions and statements. For Eve pitiably obeyed the serpent, fell from the state of original innocence, and became his slave. But the most Blessed Virgin constantly added to the gift that was originally given her, and not only never lent her ear to the serpent, but, by a power divinely received, utterly shattered his strength and power.

Therefore, they have never ceased to call the Mother of God the lily among thorns; or the earth entirely untouched, virginal, undefiled, immaculate, ever blessed and free from all contagion of sin, earth from which was formed the new Adam; a flawless, bright and fragrant paradise of innocence, immortality and delights, planted by God Himself, and fenced against every snare of the poisonous serpent; or the never-fading wood that the worm of sin has never corrupted; or the fountain ever clear and sealed by the power of the Holy Spirit; the divine temple; the treasury of immortality; or again, the unique and only daughter of life and not of death, the offshoot of grace and not of wrath, which by the singular providence of God and at variance with established and ordinary laws, flourished and flowered, although sprung from a root that was corrupt and infected.

c. Mary's Sinlessness

As if these magnificent expressions were not enough, they proclaimed in appropriate and in precise terms that where sin is treated no question whatever is to be raised concerning the holy Virgin Mary. For to her an abundance of grace was given to conquer sin completely. They also declared that the most glorious Virgin was the Reparatrix of her parents, Life-giver to posterity, chosen before the ages, prepared for Himself by the Most High and foretold by God when He said to the serpent: "I will place enmity between thee and the woman," who has undoubtedly crushed the poisonous head of the same serpent. Therefore, they affirm that the same Blessed Virgin was through grace perfectly free from every stain of sin and from all contagion of body and soul and mind; that she was always at home with God and united with Him in an eternal covenant; that she was never in darkness, but always in light; that she was, as a result, a perfectly suitable dwelling place for Christ, not because of her bodily endowments, but because of her original grace.

d. Mary's Dignity as Mother of God

. . . It was altogether proper, that, as the Only-begotten had a Father in heaven whom the Seraphim extol as thrice holy, so He should have a Mother on earth who has never lacked the splendor of holiness. As a matter of fact, this doctrine so dominated the minds and the hearts of our forefathers that a wholly extraordinary way of speaking came into vogue among them. Frequently, they referred to the Mother of God not only as immaculate but as entirely immaculate, not only as innocent but as most innocent, not only as spotless but as most spotless. They called her holy and completely removed from every stain of sin, all pure and all but the very archtype of purity and inno-cence, more beautiful than beauty, more gracious than grace, more holy than holiness, and alone holy; most pure in soul and body, who transcends all integrity and virginity, who alone and in her entirety has become the dwelling place of all the graces of the Holy Spirit, and who, God alone excepted, is superior to all, and by nature more fair, more beautiful, and more holy than the very Cherubin and Seraphim and

G

the entire angelic host; she whom all the tongues of heaven and earth cannot sufficiently extol.

e. *The Liturgy as Witness*

No one is ignorant that these forms of speech have passed almost spontaneously into the monuments of the most holy liturgy and the Office of the Church, where they often recur and are to a great extent dominant. It is here that the Mother of God is invoked and proclaimed as the one spotless dove of beauty, the rose ever blooming, perfectly pure, ever spotless and ever blessed. It is here that she is celebrated as innocence undefiled, and as the second Eve, who brought forth Emmanuel.

[There follows an account of the devotion of the faithful, of the petitions of their pastors, the convocation of a special Congregation to study the question anew, the favorable judgment of the bishops, and the final consistory of the cardinals in which Pius IX was asked "to promulgate the dogmatic definition of the Immaculate Conception of the Virgin Mother of God." The definition itself follows.]

2. THE DOGMATIC DEFINITION OF THE IMMACULATE CONCEPTION

. . . To the honor of the holy and undivided Trinity, to the glory and adornment of the Virgin Mother of God, to the exaltation of the Catholic faith, and the increase of the Catholic religion, We, by the authority of Jesus Christ our Lord, of the Blessed

Apostles, Peter and Paul, and by Our Own, declare, pronounce and define that the doctrine which holds that the Blessed Virgin Mary, at the first instant of her Conception, by a singular privilege and grace of the omnipotent God, in consideration of the merits of Jesus Christ, the Savior of mankind, was preserved free from all stain of original sin, has been revealed by God, and therefore is to be firmly and constantly believed by all the faithful.

Therefore, if any shall presume—which God forbid—to think in their hearts anything different from what has been defined by Us, let them know and realize that they are condemned by their own judgment, that they have suffered shipwreck of the faith, and have broken with the unity of the Church; moreover, if they shall dare to signify, by word or writing or any other external means what they think in their hearts, by that very fact (*facto ipso*) they subject themselves to the penalties by law established.

3. MARY, MEDIATRIX AND PATRONESS

[In a tone that recaptures something of the spirit of the Magnificat sung by the maiden whom he has just honored with the fulness of his authority as Christ's Vicar, Pius IX spontaneously calls upon the Christian world to invoke the patronage of Mary under her new title—the Immaculate Conception.]

Our speech overflows with joy, and Our tongue with exultation. We give and We shall continue to give the humblest and deepest thanks to Jesus Christ our Lord. because through His singular favor He has allowed Us, unworthy as We are, to decree and offer this honor and glory and praise to His most holy Mother. We have the surest hope and the most utter confidence that the most Blessed Virgin, who, all fair and immaculate, has crushed the poisonous head of the cruel serpent and brought salvation to the world . . . who is the safest Refuge and the most reliable Helper of all who are in danger, and the most influential Mediatrix and Conciliatrix of the whole world with her only-begotten Son . . . who has ever destroyed all heresies and delivered faithful nations and peoples from the greatest and most varied calamities . . . will through her most influential patronage graciously bring it about . . . that the guilty obtain pardon, the sick healing, the weak of heart courage, the afflicted consolation, and those in danger assistance; and that all who are in error, may, with the removal of all blindness of spirit, return to the path of truth and justice, and that there may be one flock and one shepherd.

Let all the children of the Catholic Church who are most dear to Us hear Our words, and with even more ardent zeal for piety, religion and love, continue to cherish, invoke and beseech the Blessed Virgin Mary, Mother of God, conceived without original sin, and let them with entire confidence have recourse to this sweetest Mother of grace and mercy in all dangers, difficulties, necessities, doubts and fears. For nothing need be feared, and nothing need be despaired of, so long as she is our guide, our patroness, so long as she is propitious, she our protectress. Surely, she who bears toward us the affection of a mother, and who through her interest in the affairs of all mankind is solicitous for our salvation, and who has been appointed by the Lord as Queen of heaven and earth, and has been exalted above all the choirs of the angels and the ranks of the saints, surely, she, standing at the right hand of her only-begotten Son, our Lord Jesus Christ, and with a mother's prayer, is most influential in her intercession, and obtains what she asks and cannot be denied.

Pii IX Acta, 1, 607–618 (definition in DB, 1641).

PART VIII

MARY MEDIATRIX AND CO-REDEMPTRIX

★

[Pius IX closed the *Ineffabilis Deus* with an invocation of Mary as Mediatrix and Conciliatrix of the human race. It is not surprising, then, that his successors in the pontificate should draw out in greater detail the significance of the title *Mediatrix*, a title that sums up so much of the earlier testimony of the Fathers.]

1. Leo XIII

a. *Access to the Son Through the Mother. Encyclical "Octobri Mense," 1891*

[This citation and the one that follows immediately are taken from encyclicals that foster devotion to our Lady's Rosary.]

Although the Eternal Son of God willed for the redemption and glory of man to assume the nature of man, and thereby to enter into a kind of mystical marriage with the whole human race, yet He did not do so until the absolutely free consent of His Mother-to-be was given. As Aquinas expresses it so strikingly and truly, Mary acted as it were in the person of the whole human race: "Through the Annunciation, the consent of the Virgin given in place of the whole human race was awaited" (*Sum. Theol.*, III, q. 30, a. 1). Therefore we may with no less propriety and truth affirm that we can receive absolutely nothing from that great treasury of all grace which the Lord has brought forth—since "grace and truth came through Jesus Christ" (Jn. 1:17)—nothing, unless, God so willing, it is bestowed on us through Mary. So that, just as no one can have access to the Father Most High except through the Son, so, in almost the same way, no one can have access to the Son except through the Mother.

DB, 1940 a.

b. Mediatrix to the Mediator. Encyclical "Fidentem Piumque," 1896

Now it is impossible to think of any individual who has ever contributed or ever will contribute as much service toward the reconciliation of men with God as has Mary. It was she, surely, who brought the Savior to men when they were rushing on to their eternal destruction, at the very time, that is, when, "in the place of the whole human race," she received and wondrously consented to the message which the Angel brought to earth announcing the mystery of reconciliation. She it is "of whom was born Jesus" (Mt. 1:16), she who is His true Mother and for this reason is justly regarded as *Mediatrix to the Mediator*.

DB, 1940 a.

2. Bl. Pius X: Mary, Mediatrix of all Graces. Encyclical *Ad Diem*, 1904

[This encyclical was written to commemorate the fiftieth anniversary of the definition of the Immaculate Conception. On becoming Pope, the saintly Pius X had taken as his motto: "To restore all things in Christ." Pius X dwells at length on the role that Mary plays in this work of restoration.]

a. Restoration Through Mary

For who has not discovered that there is no surer or easier way to unite all men to Christ and to obtain through Him that perfect adoption of sons, by which we become holy and immaculate in the sight of God, than through Mary? . . .

Does this mean that God could not have given us the Restorer of the human race and the Author of our faith except by way of the Virgin? Rather, it means that, since it pleased God in His eternal providence that we should have the God-Man through Mary, who conceived Him by the Holy Spirit and carried Him in her womb, there is nothing left for us but to receive Christ from the hands of Mary. For this reason, so often as prophecy is made in Holy Scripture "of the grace that will one day come to us," almost as often the Savior of men is associated with His most holy Mother. The lamb shall come forth as the ruler of earth, but from the rock of the desert; a flower shall blossom, but from the root of Jesse. It was surely Mary whom Adam saw crushing the head of the serpent, and that vision held back the tears which had welled up as a result of his condemnation. She it was whom Noah thought of when enclosed in the ark of deliverance. . . . Next to Christ it is in Mary that we find the consummation of the Law and the reality that underlies the images and the mysterious utterances of Scripture. . . .

b. Mary, Our Mother

Is not Mary the Mother of Christ? She is then our Mother too. For everyone should convince himself of this, that Jesus, who is the Word made flesh, is also the Savior of the human race. Now, as God-Man He acquired, just as other men, an individual body. But as Restorer of our race, He acquired a spiritual and mystical body—the society of those who believe in Christ. "We, the many, are one body in Christ" (Rom. 12:5). Now, the Virgin conceived the Eternal Son of God not only that He might by assuming human nature from her become a man; but that He might, through the nature assumed from her, become as well the Savior of mortal men. For this reason, the Angel announced to the shepherds: "Today there is born to you a Savior, who is Christ the Lord" (Lk. 2:11). And thus, in one and the same bosom of His most chaste Mother, Christ, at one and the same time, assumed flesh and united to Himself a spiritual body which is joined together from those "who were to believe in him" (Jn. 17:20). In this way, Mary, by bearing the Savior in her womb, can be said to have borne all those whose life was contained in the life of the Savior. All of us, therefore, who are united with

Christ and are, as the Apostle says, "members of his body, made from his flesh and his bones" (Eph. 5:30), have come forth from the womb of Mary, after the manner of a body that is joined to its head. Hence in a spiritual and mystical sense we are called the children of Mary and she is Mother of us all. "Mother indeed in spirit . . . but surely Mother of the members of Christ, which we are" (St. Aug., *de S. Virginitate*, c. 6). If, then, the most Blessed Virgin is at once the Mother of God and the Mother of men, can anyone doubt that she makes every effort that Christ, "the head of his body, the Church" (Col. 1:18), should infuse into us, His members, the gifts which are His, in order that we may above all come to know Him and to "live by him"? (1 Jn. 4:9).

c. Mary's Part in the Redemption

In order that we might live by Him, the most holy Mother of God has not only the honor of having given "the substance of her flesh to the only-begotten God about to be born of the human race" (Bede the Venerable, *In expos. in S. Lucam*, 4, 9), whereby a victim was prepared for men's salvation; hers was the task, as well, of caring for and nourishing this same Victim and even of placing It near the altar at the appointed hour. Thus, between Mother and Son there was a never-broken community of life and labor, so that to both equally apply the words of the Prophet: "My life is wasted with grief and my years in sighs" (Ps. 31:11). And when the last hour of her Son arrived, "there stood by the cross of Jesus his mother" (Jn. 19:25). Nor was she merely engaged in witnessing the cruel spectacle; rather, she rejoiced utterly that "her Only-begotten was being offered for the salvation of the human race, although her compassion was so intense that, if it were at all possible, she herself would have embraced even more eagerly all the sufferings that her Son endured. Now it is because of this community of pain and will between Mary and Christ that "she merited to become in a most worthy manner the Reparatrix of the lost world" (Eadmer of Canterbury, *De excellentia B.V.M.*, c. 9) and, therefore, the Dispenser of the totality of gifts which Jesus by His death and blood has acquired for us.

d. Mary, Dispenser of Christ's Gifts

Now surely we do not deny that the distribution of these gifts belongs by strict right to Christ personally; after all, they have been acquired for us by His death alone, and He is in His own right the Mediator between God and men. And yet, out of regard for that community of pain and suffering between Mother and Son already mentioned, the august Virgin was privileged to be "the most influential Mediatrix and Conciliatrix of the whole world with her only-begotten Son" (see above p. 88). Thus, Christ is the fountainhead, and "of his fulness we have all received" (Jn. 1:16); "from him the whole body [being closely joined and knit together through every joint of the system . . .] derives its increase to the building up of itself in love" (Eph. 4:16). But Mary, as Bernard aptly remarks, is the "aqueduct," or even the neck by which the Body is joined to the Head, and by which the Head communicates force and power to the Body. . . . It is clear, then, that we are very far from attributing to the Mother of God the power of producing supernatural grace, a power which belongs to God alone. Because, however, she transcends all others in holiness and in the intimacy of her union with Christ, and because she has been drawn by Christ into association with the work of human salvation, she merits for us congruously, as they say, what Christ merited for us condignly, and she is the principal Minister of the graces to be distributed. He "has taken his seat at the right hand of the Majesty on high" (Heb. 1:3). But Mary as Queen stands at His right hand, "the safest Refuge and the most reliable Helper of all who are in danger, so that nothing need be feared, nothing need be despaired of, so long as she is our guide, she our patroness, so long as she is propitious, she our protectress" (Pius IX, *Ineffabilis Deus*).

Pii X Acta (1905), 150–155.

3. BENEDICT XV: MARY AS CO-REDEMPTRIX. APOSTOLIC LETTER *Inter Sodalicia*, 1918

[Benedict XV in this apostolic letter does not use the title *co-Redemptrix* but expresses the idea quite vividly.[7]]

[7] On June 26, 1913, the Congregation of the Holy Office praised the practice of adding to the name of Jesus the name "of His Mother, the Blessed Mary, as our co-Redemptrix" (AAS, 5 [1913], 364). Some six months later, January 22, 1914, the same Congrega-

Thus, she [Mary] suffered and all but died along with her Son suffering and dying; thus, for the salvation of men she abdicated the rights of a mother towards her Son, and insofar as it was hers to do, she immolated the Son to placate God's justice, so that she herself may justly be said to have redeemed together with Christ the human race.

AAS, 10 (1918), 182.

4. Pius XI: Mary's Offering on Calvary. Encyclical *Miserentissimus Redemptor*, 1928

[At the close of the Holy Year of 1933, Pius XI invoked Mary publicly under the title "co-Redemptrix." In the following passage from the encyclical on the Sacred Heart, the same Pontiff portrays Mary as actually offering her Son on Calvary. This same idea will be repeated by Pius XII in his encyclical on the Mystical Body. Therefore a word of caution is in order. Although Mary associated herself with the offering of her Son, this affective oblation formed no part of that great liturgical offering on Calvary in which Christ alone was Priest and Victim. Thus, it is only Christ who paid by way of sacrifice the actual price of our redemption. It is only Christ who merited our justification in the strict sense of the term (*de condigno*). Mary, to quote Benedict XV, immolated her Son "insofar as it was hers to do" (see above). In the words of Pius X, Mary "merits for us congruously (*de congruo*) . . . what Christ merited for us condignly" (*de condigno;* see above, p. 96).]

---

tion enriched with an indulgence a prayer in which the Blessed Virgin Mary was referred to as "co-Redemptrix of the human race" (AAS, 6 [1914] 108; cf. DB, 1978a, and note).

May the most gracious Mother of God be propitious to these our wishes and these our undertakings; she who by giving us Christ the Redeemer, and by rearing Him, and by offering Him at the foot of the Cross as Victim for our sins, by such intimate association with Christ, and by her own most singular grace, became and is affectionately known as Reparatrix. Confident of her intercession with Christ, who alone is Mediator of God and men, and who willed to associate His Mother with Himself as the Advocate of sinners, as the Dispenser and Mediatrix of grace, we impart . . . the apostolic blessing.

AAS, 20 (1928), 178.

5. Pius XII: Mary, Mother of the Mystical Body. Encyclical *Mystici Corporis*, 1943

[The portrait of Mary as Mediatrix and her role in the Redemption is beautifully summarized by Pius XII in the concluding prayer of his encyclical on the Mystical Body.]

127. Venerable Brothers, may the Virgin Mother of God grant the prayers of Our paternal heart—and they are yours too—and obtain for all a true love of the Church. Her sinless soul was filled with the divine Spirit of Jesus Christ, more than all other created souls; and "in the place of the whole human race," she gave her consent for a "spiritual marriage between the Son of God and human nature" (*Sum. Theol.*, III, q. 30, a. 1). Within her virginal womb Christ our

Lord already bore the exalted title of Head of the Church; in a marvelous birth she brought Him forth as source of all supernatural life, and presented Him, newborn, as Prophet, King and Priest to those who were the first come of Jews and Gentiles to adore Him. Her only Son, yielding to a mother's prayer "in Cana of Galilee," performed the miracle by which "his disciples believed in him" (Jn. 2:11). Free from all sin, original and personal, always most intimately united with her Son, as another Eve she offered Him on Golgotha to the Eternal Father for all the children of Adam sin-stained by his fall, and her mother's rights and mother's love were included in the holocaust.

128. Thus she who corporally was the Mother of our Head, through the added title of pain and glory became spiritually the Mother of all His members. She it was who through her powerful prayers obtained the grace that the Spirit of our divine Redeemer, already given to the Church on the Cross, should be bestowed through miraculous gifts on the newly-founded hierarchy on Pentecost. Bearing with courage and confidence the tremendous burden of her sorrows and desolation, truly the Queen of martyrs, she more than all the faithful "filled up those things that are wanting of the sufferings of Christ . . . for his body, which is the Church" (Col. 1:24); and she continued to show for the Mystical Body of Christ, born from the pierced Heart of the Savior, the same mother's care

and ardent love with which she clasped the Infant Jesus to her warm and nourishing breast.

129. May she, then, the most holy Mother of all Christ's members, to whose Immaculate Heart We have trustingly consecrated all men, her body and soul refulgent with the glory of heaven where she reigns with her Son—may she never cease to beg from Him that a continuous flow of graces may pass from its glorious Head into all the members of the Mystical Body. May she throw about the Church today, as in times gone by, the mantle of her protection and obtain from God that now at last the Church and all mankind may enjoy more peaceful days.

AAS, 35 (1943), 247–48 [tr. with some changes from the Paulist Press edition].

PART IX

THE DOGMA OF THE ASSUMPTION

Pius XII: Apostolic Constitution *Munificentis-simus Deus*, Nov. 1, 1950

[Shortly after the proclamation of the dogma of the Immaculate Conception the Holy See was besieged with petitions for the definition of the Assumption of our Lady. Not a few of the Fathers gathered at the Vatican Council (1870) made the same request of Pius IX.[8] Since that time and up to the year 1941, the dogmatic definition of Mary's Assumption was requested by 113 cardinals, over 300 archbishops and bishops, some 32,000 priests and brothers, 50,000 religious women, and by more than 8,000,000 of the laity. On May 1, 1946, the following questionnaire was sent to all the bishops of the Catholic world: "Do you, Venerable Brethren, in view of the wis-

---

[8] The Fathers at the Vatican Council gave the following reason for their request: "According to the teaching of the Apostle [Rom. 5:8; I Cor. 15:24, 26, 54, 57; Heb. 2:14, and other texts], when Jesus triumphed over the ancient serpent, He gained a three-fold victory over sin and its consequences, i.e., over concupiscence and death. Since the Mother of God is associated in a special way with her Son in this triumph (Gen. 3:15), and this in accord with the unanimous teaching of the Fathers, we have no doubt that in the above-mentioned passage (Gen. 3:15) this same Blessed Virgin is foretold as illustrious by a similar victory that is threefold: over sin by her Immaculate Conception, over concupiscence by her virginal motherhood, and, in like manner, over death by a triumphant resurrection similar to that of her Son" (*The Vatican Council, Collectio Lacensis*, VII, 860).

H   101

dom and prudence that is yours, judge that the bodily Assumption of the most Blessed Virgin can be proposed and defined as a dogma of faith; and do you along with your clergy and people desire it?" (from the present constitution). Pius XII assures us that the reply to both questions was "almost unanimous." In the section of the constitution that we shall open with, the Supreme Pontiff draws the inevitable conclusion from the consent of those whom "the Holy Spirit has placed as bishops to rule the Church of God" (Acts 20:28).]

1. THE CONSENT OF THE BISHOPS

12. . . . Thus, from the universal consent of the ordinary magisterium of the Church a certain and firm argument is drawn, by which confirmation is given that the bodily Assumption of the Blessed Virgin Mary into heaven—which, surely, insofar as it refers to the actual "glorification" in heaven of the virginal body of the beloved Mother of God, no faculty of the human mind could know by its own natural powers— is a truth revealed by God, and is, therefore, to be believed with steadfast faith and fidelity by all the Church's sons. For, as the same Vatican Council again asserts: "All those truths are to be believed with divine and Catholic faith which are contained in the word of God, written or handed down, and which the Church, either by a solemn judgment, or by her ordinary and universal magisterium, proposes for belief as having been divinely revealed" (On Divine Faith, ch. 3 [DB, 1792]).

2. THE ARGUMENT FROM TRADITION

13. Various testimonies, indications and traces of this accepted faith of the Church are clearly manifest through the course of the centuries from the most remote periods. And the same faith is revealed from day to day in ever clearer light.

a. The Belief of the Faithful

14. True, Christ's faithful, under the instruction and guidance of their pastors, learned from the Sacred Books that the Virgin Mary, during her earthly pilgrimage, lived a life subject to anxiety, difficulties, poverty, and suffering; they learned, too, that what the saintly old man Simeon had foretold actually came to pass, namely, that a sharp sword pierced her heart at the Cross of her Divine Son and our Redeemer. Similarly, the faithful found no difficulty in admitting that the great Mother of God had departed this life, just as had her only-begotten Son. But this in no way stopped them from believing and professing openly that her sacred body was never subject to the corruption of the grave, that the sacred tabernacle of the Divine Word was never resolved into mouldering dust. On the contrary, enlightened by divine grace and moved by filial piety towards her, the Mother of God and our own sweet Mother, they contemplated with ever-increasing clarity the marvelous harmony and interrelation of those privileges which an all-provident God had lavished on this beloved associate

of our Redeemer; privileges which reached so lofty a peak that, apart from the human nature of Jesus Christ, no creature of God other than she has ever attained them.

b. The Liturgy as Witness

17. In the liturgical books which deal with the feast either of the "Dormition" or of the "Assumption of holy Mary," expressions are used which lend a certain harmony to their testimony that when the Virgin Mother of God was passing from this earthly exile to the regions above, a decree of God's providence saw to it that her body was treated in a way that befitted her dignity as Mother of the Incarnate Word, and the other privileges with which she was endowed. To use an outstanding example, this idea is found in the *Sacramentary* which Our Predecessor of eternal memory, Hadrian I [772–795], sent to the Emperor Charlemagne. There we read: "Sacred to us, O Lord, is this day's festival, whereon the Holy Mother of God suffered death for a time, and yet could not be held down by death's bonds, she who brought forth incarnate from herself Thy Son and our Lord" (*The Gregorian Sacramentary* [PL, 78, 133]).

18. . . . In the Byzantine liturgy, as well, the bodily Assumption of Mary the Virgin is time and again associated not only with her dignity as Mother of God but also with other privileges, and in a very special way with her virginal motherhood, granted her by the singular design of a provident God: "Upon thee, God,

the King of the universe, has bestowed gifts which transcend nature. For just as He guarded thy virginity in childbirth, so too did He keep thy body incorrupt in the sepulchre, and by His divine power transfer and glorify it" (*Months of the Whole Year* [*Menaea totius anni*, Jul.-Aug., Vol. 6, Romae, 1901]).

c. The Feast in the Roman Church

19. Moreover, the Apostolic See, which is heir to the office entrusted to the Prince of the Apostles of confirming the brethren in the faith, has by its own authority made the celebration of this feast ever more solemn, and, in doing so, has surely and effectively aroused the eager minds of Christ's faithful to an ever deeper appreciation of the importance of the mystery commemorated. Thus, the feast of the Assumption was raised in dignity, from the rank that it held from the beginning in common with other feasts of Mary, to the rank of the more solemn feasts of the whole liturgical cycle. Again, Our Predecessor, St. Sergius I [680–701], in prescribing the Litany—or, as it is called, the Stational Procession—to be recited on the four major feasts of Mary, enumerates along with the feast of the Nativity, the Annunciation, and the Purification the feast of "the Dormition of Mary the Virgin" (*Liber Pontificalis* [ed. Duchesne, 1, 376]). Later, St. Leo IV [847–855] saw to it that the feast which by that time was celebrated under the title of the Assumption of the Blessed Mother of God should be commemorated with even greater solemnity. This he

did by ordering a vigil to be kept before the feast.
and prayers to be said through the octave following
(*ibid.*, 2, 110). And willingly seizing the occasion
offered, he himself agreed to take part in the celebration, surrounded by a great multitude of the faithful.
Moreover, evidence that the observance of a holy fast
for the day before the feast was prescribed from
ancient times is convincingly shown from the testimony of Our Predecessor, St. Nicholas I [858–867],
who deals with the principal fasts "which the Holy
Roman Church has received from antiquity and ob-
serves to this day" (*Replies of Nicholas I to the In-
quiries of the Bulgarians* [Mansi, 15, 403]).

d. The Fathers as Witness

20. The liturgy of the Church, however, does not
engender the Catholic faith, but rather flows from it;
the sacred rites of our religion grow out of our faith
as fruit from the tree. For this reason the Holy Fathers
and the great Doctors, in the homilies and sermons
they delivered to the people on this festival, did not
draw this doctrine from the feast as from its primary
source; they spoke of it, rather, as a doctrine already
known and accepted by Christ's faithful. They set it
forth with greater clarity; they explained its meaning
in reality with more profound arguments, setting
forth especially in fuller light what the liturgical
books often sketched only in outline, that is, that by
this feast we commemorate not only the fact that the
Blessed Virgin Mary's body suffered no corruption

when separated from her soul, but also the fact of its victory over death and its heavenly "glorification," after the example of her only-begotten Jesus Christ.

21. Thus, St. John Damascene, who far excels all others as herald of this traditional truth, comparing the bodily Assumption of God's beloved Mother with her other gifts and privileges, delivers these eloquent words: "There was need that the body of her who in childbirth had preserved her virginity intact, be preserved incorrupt after death. There was need that she who had carried her Creator as a babe on her bosom, should linger lovingly in the dwelling of her God. There was need that the bride whom the Father had betrothed to Himself should live in the bridal chamber of heaven, that she who had looked so closely upon her very own Son on the Cross, and who there felt in her heart the sword-pangs of sorrow which in bearing Him she had been spared, should look upon Him seated with His Father. There was need that God's Mother should enter into her Son's possessions, and, as Mother of God and handmaid, be reverenced by all creation" (*On the Falling Asleep of the Mother of God*, 2, 14 [PG, 96, 740–41]).

e. The Assumption in the Old Testament

25. Many theologians and sacred orators illustrate their belief in the Assumption by freely borrowing words and incidents from the Sacred Scriptures, after the example of the Holy Fathers. Thus, to recall only a few instances of this usage, some adduce the words

of the Psalmist: "Arise, O Lord, into thy resting place: thou and the ark which thou hast sanctified" (Ps. 131:8). In the ark of the covenant, made of incorruptible wood and placed in the temple of God, they see a figure of the most pure body of the Virgin Mary preserved free from any corruption of the grave and carried aloft to the exalted glory of heaven. In the same way, when dealing with this subject, they portray our Queen as entering triumphantly into the royal court of heaven and taking her seat at the right hand of the Divine Redeemer (see Ps. 44:10, 14–16). Likewise, they adduce the bride of the Canticle, "who goeth up by the desert, as a pillar of smoke, of aromatical spices, of myrrh, and frankincense," to be crowned with a diadem (Cant. 3:6; see 4:8, 6:9). These passages they set forth as figures of that heavenly Queen and heavenly Bride, who along with the Divine Bridegroom was carried aloft to the court of heaven.

f. The Assumption in the New Testament

27. In addition, the Scholastic Doctors have seen the Assumption of the Virgin Mother of God signified not only in various figures of the Old Testament but also in the woman clothed with the sun, whom the Apostle John beheld on the island of Patmos (Apoc. 12:1 ff.). Again, from the passages of the New Testament they chose for especially careful consideration the words: "Hail, full of grace, the Lord is with thee, blessed art thou among women" (Lk.

1:28). For they saw in the mystery of the Assumption the achievement of that fulness of grace bestowed on the Blessed Virgin, and her extraordinary benediction that countered Eve's malediction.

28. For this reason, at the very dawn of Scholastic theology, the saintly Bishop Amadeus of Lausanne [1144–1159] affirms that the flesh of Mary the Virgin remained incorrupt—for it is incredible that her body should have seen corruption—since surely it was united again to her soul, and together with it was crowned with glory in the court of heaven. "For she was full of grace and blessed among women" (Lk. 1:28). She alone merited to conceive the true God of true God, whom she bore as a virgin, as a virgin suckled, fondling Him on her lap, and to whose needs she ministered with loving devotedness" (*On the Death of the Blessed Virgin, Her Assumption into Heaven, and Exaltation at Her Son's Right Hand* [PL, 188, 1337]).

29. [The theme of Mary as Ark of the Covenant is repeated by St. Anthony of Padua. Commenting on the text: "Arise, O Lord, into thy resting place, thou and the ark which thou hast sanctified" (Ps. 131:8), he makes the following application to Mary: "The ark of sanctification arose as well, when on this day the Virgin Mother was taken up to the heavenly chamber" (*On the Solemnity of the Blessed Virgin Mary* [Padua, 1855], p. 51).]

30–35. [The witness of the great theologians and Doctors of the Church: St. Albert the Great, St.

Thomas Aquinas, St. Bonaventure, St. Bernardine of Siena, St. Robert Bellarmine, St. Francis of Sales and St. Alphonsus Liguori.]

g. The Faith of the Church

36. Since the mystery celebrated in this feast had already been set forth in its full light, there have been not a few Doctors who, rather than treat of the theological arguments which prove how thoroughly fitting and reasonable it is to believe the bodily Assumption of the Blessed Virgin Mary into heaven, turned their attention and genius to the faith of the Church, the mystical Bride of Christ who has neither spot nor wrinkle (see Eph. 5:27), who indeed is hailed by the Apostle as "the pillar and foundation of truth" (I Tim. 3:15). Relying on this accepted faith, they regarded any contrary opinion as rash, if not heretical. In fact, St. Peter Canisius, among many others, after declaring that the very word *Assumption* means the "glorification" not only of the soul but also of the body, and that the Church for many centuries had celebrated the mystery of Mary's Assumption in this sense, makes the following observation: "This view has obtained in the Church for some centuries, and has been so deeply imprinted in the hearts of the devout and so commended by the whole Church, that those who deny the Assumption of Mary's body into heaven are not even to be given a polite hearing; rather they are to be hissed down everywhere as men who are at best obstinate, or altogether rash, and

imbued with a spirit more heretical than Catholic"
(*On Mary the Virgin* [*Summa Aurea*, Bourasse-
Migne, 9, 70]).

37. At the same time, the Pre-eminent Doctor
[Suarez, *Doctor Eximius*], after acknowledging this
norm of Mariology: "The mysteries of grace which
God has worked in the Virgin are to be measured not
by ordinary laws, but by God's omnipotence, supposing, of course, the rules of propriety and the absence
of any contradiction or incompatibility with Scripture" (*In 3am Partem D. Thomae*, q. 27, a. 2, disp. 3,
sect. 5, n. 31); and relying on the accepted faith of
the Church, could conclude, so far as the mystery of
the Assumption is concerned, that this mystery was to
be believed with the same steadfastness of mind as the
Immaculate Conception of the Blessed Virgin. And
even at that time he judged that mysteries of this
nature could be defined.

h. The Pontiff's Own Encomium

38. All these arguments and considerations of the
Holy Fathers and theologians are based on the Sacred
Scriptures as on their ultimate foundation. Indeed, the
Scriptures set before our eyes, as it were, God's
gracious Mother in most intimate association with her
Divine Son, and ever sharing in His destiny. Therefore, it seems all but impossible to see her who conceived, who bore, who nursed Him with her own
milk, who held Him in her embrace and pressed Him
to her breast, now, after her life on earth, separated

from Him, if not in soul, yet in body. Since our Redeemer is the Son of Mary, surely He who observed the divine Law most perfectly could hardly fail to honor, besides His Eternal Father, His most beloved Mother. And since it was within His power to adorn her with the great honor of keeping her untouched by the corruption of the grave, we must believe that He did so.

39. We must especially recall that, from the second century on, the Holy Fathers portrayed the Virgin Mary in the role of the new Eve, subject surely to the new Adam, but intimately associated in that struggle with the enemy of hell, which, as the Proto-Gospel foretells, was to result in complete victory over sin and death, two realities which are constantly coupled in the writings of the Apostle to the Gentiles (see Rom. 5:6; I Cor. 15:21–26, 54–47). Therefore, just as the glorious resurrection of Christ was an essential element of this victory and its crowning memorial, so too the struggle that was common to the Blessed Virgin and to her Son was to be brought to a close with the "glorification" of her virginal body. For, as the same Apostle says, "When . . . mortality puts on immortality, then shall come to pass the word that is written: Death is swallowed up in victory" (I Cor. 15:54).

40. Therefore, the venerable Mother of God, united with Jesus Christ in a mysterious way from all eternity "in one and the same decree" of predestination, in her Conception immaculate, a virgin inviolate in her divine

motherhood, a noble associate of the Divine Redeemer, who won complete victory over sin and its consequences, received at last the supreme culmination of her privileges: to be preserved free from the corruption of the sepulchre, and, like her Son before her, with death vanquished, to be carried aloft in body and soul to the exalted glory of heaven, and there as Queen to be resplendent at the right hand of her very own Son, the immortal King of the ages (see I Tim. 1:17).

3. THE DOGMATIC DEFINITION OF THE ASSUMPTION

44. Therefore, after directing unceasing prayers of petition to God, and after invoking the light of the Spirit of Truth, to the glory of the omnipotent God who lavished His special benevolence on Mary the Virgin, to the honor of her Son, the immortal King of the ages and Victor over sin and death, to the increase in glory of this same venerable Mother, and to the joy and exultation of the whole Church, We, by the authority of our Lord Jesus Christ, of the Blessed Apostles Peter and Paul, and Our Own, pronounce, declare and define it to be a dogma divinely revealed, that the Immaculate Mother of God, the ever Virgin Mary, when the course of her earthly life was run, was assumed in body and in soul to heavenly glory.

45. Therefore, if anyone, which God forbid, shall willingly dare either to deny or to call into question what has been defined by Us, let him know that he has utterly abandoned divine and Catholic faith.

[After three concluding paragraphs the apostolic constitution is signed and sealed by Pius XII. The signatures of the thirty-eight cardinals who were present are also affixed.]

AAS, 32 (1950), 753–771 [Paragraph numbers, dates and more explicit references are the editor's].

TITLES OF MARY

★

INDEX

★